BREATHE
GOLF

THE MISSING LINK TO A
WINNING PERFORMANCE

JAYNE STOREY

BREATHE GOLF

First published in 2019 by

Panoma Press Ltd
48 St Vincent Drive, St Albans, Herts, AL1 5SJ, UK
info@panomapress.com
www.panomapress.com

Book layout by Neil Coe.

Printed on acid-free paper from managed forests.

ISBN 978-1-784521-57-8

Cover image shows the Chinese symbol for "chi" which means life-force, energy or breath.

DEDICATION

In loving memory of my wonderful Mum
who had a radiant joy and enthusiasm for life
and always encouraged me to follow my own path.

COMMENTARY

I first met Jayne in 2015 when I approached her for a coaching lesson. At the time I was interested in understanding more about her teachings and in the possible inclusion of her methods in Adam's upcoming golf app, Pin.

What immediately struck me was the realness, simplicity and authenticity of her approach, the opposite of that which is often provided in the commercial golf industry.

While those at the top of the game have improved dramatically due to the increased knowledge and understanding of what helps to develop elite athletic and sporting performance, plus of course all the technological advances in equipment and the amount of time the tour professionals spend practising and working at their game, the story is not the same for the everyday golfer who plays and loves golf.

Regardless – or maybe because – of the endless conveyor belt of new fads and gimmicks, from something you can strap to your wrist to a sexy new driver that can add 20 yards to the average tee shot, the performance of the amateur player is essentially just the same as it was when I started in golf 40 years ago. In spite of the unprecedented improvements in knowledge of teachers and coaches within the industry, and the tools to impart this knowledge, improvement has proven elusive.

With this in mind – for surely improvement fosters enjoyment – what Jayne practises, preaches and teaches about the quiet mind is clearly an important facet of golf and such an interesting subject that I believe it would behove all players to embrace it. Far better for the average player, who often has to juggle work and family commitments with a very limited amount of golf practice time, to devote some time to a skill that will allow his or her other skills to develop.

The quiet mind, the zone if you like, is one facet of golf that the top professionals and club amateurs can share.

A new approach is timely, to encourage more enjoyment and more participation in the game.

I've enjoyed reading the book and will keep referring to it.

Phil Scott

migolfclub.com

WHAT OTHERS ARE SAYING

"Jayne brings together both the mental and physical aspects of eastern methodologies that result not only in game improvement but also the ability to take it to the course under pressure and perform at a high level. Her work is unique in that all 'instructors' focus either on swing theory or 'getting into the zone' but Jayne very naturally combines both into a practical process that improves all aspects. These are centuries-old techniques adapted to the demands of today's high-performance athlete."

John Killian, 1.6 hdcp, Hong Kong

"Jayne teaches the practical application of mindfulness in sport, specifically how mind and movement should complement each other to allow performance to emerge. Her work is a bridge between technical coaching and performance, allowing golfers to take swing concepts and turn them into effective motion."

Karl Morris, Founder, The Mind Factor

"Jayne's work takes the mental side of golf and enhances the results so that you have the ability to relax, clear your mind and perform without a personal critic. As an amateur high-handicap player, there are many shots which I will not produce on any given round of golf. The ability to leave these shots behind is very important, and Jayne provides a method of accomplishing this."

Benson Dale Pilloff, 25 hdcp, North Carolina, USA

"There are two spheres of golf instruction: one is physical and the other is mental; and yet both of these approaches supposedly involve thinking. Jayne Storey's unique approach teaches golfers how to 'not think'. She is the spiritual teacher of golf, showing us how to be present on the course."

Jim Horn, 12.6 hdcp, British Columbia, Canada

"Jayne's approach to combining the elements and disciplines of Tai Chi within golf is hugely beneficial and provides a definite 'missing link' to improvement within the game."

Nicky Lawrenson, LPGA Professional

"Jayne's teaching applies ancient concepts of meditation, breathing and movement to the benefit of your golf. Her instruction provides a link between the mind and body, allowing the mental and technical sides to be combined and applied naturally and athletically. While the mental game takes the golfer tantalisingly to the door of 'the zone', Jayne opens the door to lead you through and beyond."

John Mather, 4 hdcp, Northumberland, UK

"To play golf without the brain being cluttered with technical swing thoughts is to play effortless golf, but there is a bigger picture here, which Jayne's coaching influences. Emotional control on a golf course is vital to playing at your very best, for professionals and amateurs alike, and Jayne teaches how to play without tension or fear."

Tom Brisbane, 7 hdcp, St Ives, UK

"A breath of fresh air in golf writing… at last!"

Christopher Peters, 16 hdcp, Cumbria

"Chi-Performance GOLF transcends golf technique; it will bring you closer to golfing nirvana than any six-pack of instructors ever could. Provided you have the golfing fundamentals from a minimum three years playing, and you make Jayne's method 80% of your training, you are guaranteed to reach golfing paradise."

Peter Fitzgerald, 6 hdcp, Kildare, Ireland

"Jayne Storey's approach will soon be as fundamental to the game as the grip and set-up."

Michael Wharton-Palmer, 9-time Arkansas State title winner

"If performance is 'potential minus interference', Jayne's coaching enables a golfer to realise their full potential by releasing the use of their fundamental movement skills in a very natural, non-technical way. Moreover, she helps the golfer to maximise the use of these natural skills by enabling them to ignore the negative interference from their inner voice, again through proven, non-technical methods."

Mike Snapes, 6 hdcp, Essex

"Ancient wisdom like this must be remembered and integrated into our lives and games. As a golf professional with more than 30 years of coaching experience, I can confirm that the benefits to be gained from Jayne's approach are immediate, permanent and far-reaching."

Peter Millhouse, Head Coach, La Reserva de Sotogrande

"Jayne's approach is a breath of fresh air, along with a fantastic insight to marrying the mind and the body and a freeing up of the mind through the breath. She has brought a transformation to the game of unreal proportion but only for those that have the mindset to see it, as she is clearly ahead of her time. This game we try to master, Storey holds the key that unlocks our ability to perform."

Alan O'Meara, PGA Ireland

"Jayne's teachings on breathing and meditation techniques have helped me enormously, not only to play better golf but also to enjoy my game a lot more. Her advice is invaluable to all inexperienced high handicappers like me!"

Toni Crutchley, 36 hdcp, Birmingham

"Every now and then someone comes along that makes a difference, seeing things from a fresh perspective, adding new meaning, achieving creativity out of knowledge and bringing inspirational new material to a well-known field. Jayne Storey is such a figurehead. The golfer now has an opportunity for change and improvement in a unique way that also manages the whole person rather than any individual part. I highly recommend you take any and every opportunity to work with Jayne using any of her programmes."

Peter Hudson, President, World Golf Teacher's Federation (GB&I)

"I have dropped four shots off my golf game in the last three weeks by following your advice to play golf one breath at a time, one shot at a time, one hole at a time. Brilliant!"

Adrian Henshaw, 15 hdcp, Coventry

ACKNOWLEDGEMENTS

With love and thanks to my father for his help with the proofreading and layout of the material herein; and to my sister for all the laughs and pep talks, especially since Mum's been gone.

This book would also not have been possible without the help of the following people, each of whom have my sincere thanks.

Joan and David Taylor

Rod Phillips

Françoise Emery

Kevin Bryant

Richard Simmons

Neil Davidson

Suzanne and Jon Scott-Maxwell

Erik Anggard

Heather Newham

Brigid Marlin

John Goody

Natasha and Dieter Jobst

FOREWORD

We now seem to live in a world of 'instant experts' and 'YouTube influencers': people who have very little actual experience in the field in which they claim to have expertise. It would now appear that the idea of actually doing the groundwork and applying your craft in the real world is as quaint as a landline telephone.

In my opinion this is a tragedy, as we are losing the importance of true skill and applied knowledge in the face of instant fads and fixes. The reason I mention this at the start is that you are about to read a book by a genuine expert in her field, someone who has actually immersed herself in the practice she coaches. For years and years the work has gone on. Jayne Storey has studied, practised and implemented meditation and Tai Chi in competitive sports for a number of decades. She has spent time at the coalface working with students to become a master of her craft. In today's world this is becoming increasingly rare.

The book you are about to read has beneath it a foundation of ancient wisdom combined with modern scientific verification.

Those who dare to teach must never be afraid to keep learning and Jayne is a perfect example of this, as she has spent so much time researching and verifying the ideas, tools and techniques you are about to read.

Within the game of golf, I have often said we are *drowning in information but searching for knowledge*. We seem to be heading further into the abyss of technical overload and – as you will understand while you read this wonderful book – we just cannot perform with a head full of technical instructions.

Yet do not confuse the simplicity of the approach regarding the application of the breath to golf with its potential to be effective.

I have been lucky enough to work with some of the world's best golfers and believe me, under the white heat of major championship golf you need to be able to control your attention, and to own your golf swing as well as your individual, specific processes.

One of the things I always ask top players is to *give me a description of your state of mind when you have played your very best golf, the days when the game seems easy and effortless and you can release your true and authentic capability.*

So many times the reply has been to the effect that their mind was 'still' or very 'calm'. As Jayne will confirm within this book it is less thought we need and not more, especially when we're under pressure to perform.

This state of a calm, quiet and yet attentive mind is good not only for your golf but also for your life in general, as we increasingly live in a world of constant low-level distraction.

You may not have thought about practising meditation in its formal sense, or perhaps you've toyed with the idea but don't really know how to begin; but it is my strong belief that golf can be your go-to place to practise this ancient art, as the benefits for your game can and will be profound.

You will also no doubt take many of the wise words within the book and begin to apply them on a much wider scale as they can doubtless help you to improve at all levels, from your business to your relationships and your overall wellbeing.

Immerse yourself in the content and rest assured you are being taken on a journey by someone who not only has your best interests at heart, but has a body of knowledge that is unique. I place you in the safe hands of Jayne Storey and hope you enjoy your journey through the book as much as I did.

Karl Morris
themindfactor.com

CONTENTS

"Ye see ... merely shootin' par is second best. Goin' for results like that leads men and cultures and entire worlds astray. But if ye do it from the inside ye get the results eventually and everythin' else along with it. So ye will na' see me givin' people many tips about the gowf swings lik' they do in all the 'how-to' books. I will na' do it. Ye must start from the inside ..."

Michael Murphy, *Golf in the Kingdom*

INTRODUCTION

The keys to the effortless golf shot lie in the moments of stillness before movement occurs.

In fact, the perfect shot has less to do with your understanding of swing technique and more to do with how well you breathe, and the connection this awareness fosters between your mind and body by quietening the internal dialogue, reducing anxiety and allowing for fluidity of motion.

The innate intelligence of the mind-body connection, which manifests as 'the zone' or flow, can best be activated when the attention follows the breath, but this condition cannot be forced: it can only be trained.

This book is about the training required: the practice of breath-centred meditation, which alone can help us to access the unique experience of relaxed concentration, the coveted Zen-mind, which parallels the zone.

Yet while observing the breath may sound like a simple thing, it certainly isn't easy, especially considering the restless nature of our attention and the dominant energies of the mind and ego, neither of which have anything to do with hitting the perfect golf shot. The truth is that these things are more of a hindrance than a help.

Looking back over the many years of work and research into how awareness of the breath can influence movement shows that my personal story and my quest for understanding are intimately entwined.

It all began 31 years ago when I started training, studying and teaching the Chinese *internal* martial arts, of which Tai Chi is the most well-known; and during this whole time I have been captivated by the relationship between breathing, internal stillness and the manifestation of fluid motion.

It wasn't always so.

When I was a child, teenager and young woman I was so shy, introverted, and painfully self-conscious that I would hide in my room behind a book, day and night, and I couldn't enjoy the wonderful opportunities like swimming, tennis, figure skating, judo, horse riding and guitar lessons that my parents gave to my sister and me when we were children.

There is a thin line between being self-conscious and becoming self-aware. Crossing that line has been a lifetime's journey. What I've discovered is how difficult (nigh on impossible) it is to function well in any endeavour while anxious or nervous, but once the keys to mastering this have been trained (the components of which are revealed in this book) it allows for effortless performance in all situations where pressure is a factor.

However, this is not just another book about 'performing under pressure': it is specifically about performing complex movement skills in the unique and intense high-pressure situation of competition.

In this case we're looking at the golf swing although the principles apply equally well to the tennis serve, the penalty kick, the 100m sprint, the triple-salchow jump, the half-pipe routine, dancing and playing the violin – all when the individual is performing against opponents, in front of a crowd or a panel of judges.

In 1987, when I was in my early twenties, I saw an advert in London's *Time Out* magazine for a Tai Chi class and I instinctively knew that it would give me a centre-point for my life, something to anchor me and hold on to, something to make me stronger. I started training because I believed that if I could begin to feel at home in my body then I would be more confident.

From the first class I was introduced to a world of stillness, movement and the aesthetics of power from the slow, relaxed grace of the

Tai Chi form to the explosive dynamism of kung fu. I remember being obsessed for two whole years trying to learn the beautiful yet devastating 'Dragon Fist' of Chinese boxing (Hsing Yi), which I would watch on VHS video on the TV in the houseshare where I was living, before going outside into the garden to practise for hours on end.

Since then, movement has been my passion, daily practice, way of life and now my career. I have been fascinated by athletic and artistic motion, devouring everything in the sporting calendar, from the Oxford-Cambridge Boat Race, Wimbledon and the World Cup, to the Open Championship, Athletics Diamond League and the Winter Olympics. I've also watched countless classical music concerts, ballet and contemporary dance performances – all with an eye that's been gradually trained over the decades to see the relationship between stillness and movement in the performer.

Why is it, I have wondered, that an elite golfer, gymnast, figure skater or violinist can deliver perfect movement in practice or rehearsal but then fail to deliver this same fluidity and exactness of motion when under pressure? How can the centuries-old principles of Tai Chi and its teachings about the mind, the breath and movement help to solve this riddle?

This book is not just an attempt to answer these questions, but to look at what the questions ask of the performer. What changes in the golfer, the gymnast or the musician to warrant a sometimes dramatic change in their ability to move with fluidity during performance? Yes, nerves, anxiety and pressure come into play, but what exactly does that mean, how is it manifested in the body and then translated into movement and what can be done to reverse the sometimes devastating consequences of failing to perform at one's best when it really matters?

Of all sports, golf lends itself particularly well to the eastern approach on offer here with myriad similarities between the game and Tai Chi, not least of which is the starting point from stillness into explosive movement, the use of ground forces and lower-body stability, joint-stacking, torque and rotation, leverage, hitting through the target and above all, the necessity for a quiet mind.

When I first started to explore the game I was amazed at how closely aligned it is to martial arts principles, but I also saw how it lacked some basic teachings that can serve as the foundation upon which a reliable and repeatable golf swing could be built. These teachings include the biomechanics of structure and relaxed power; the use of the breath for controlling anxiety and reducing mental interference; and of course the imperative of training the mind-body connection that doesn't yet feature in the mainstream approach, which even in the early 21st century is still for the most part divided into technical instruction or mental game coaching.

For the last seven years I've been working on how to bring the eastern principles of the mind-body connection to golfers across the world in the form of detailed, written instruction, having worked on the method itself (**Chi-Performance GOLF**) since 2002.

With countless drafts and rewriting of the material, it became apparent that the ancient principles around breathing needed to be examined and presented as the fundamental prerequisite, the basic training for all competitive golfers who want to enjoy more effortless shots and, above all, know how to recreate the internal conditions that will allow for the perfect shot to manifest when they're under pressure.

Yet the teachings about the breath, rooted as they are in the spiritual traditions of the eastern world, must be approached with sincerity by teacher and student alike in acknowledgement of the timeless truths that were originally presented to humanity 2,500 years ago by Gautama Buddha.

Problems can never be resolved at the same level on which they are created, so the need arises to seek answers beyond the ordinary, everyday realms of the mind and ego. So often we see centuries-old principles watered down, made easier or more palatable to suit the western attitude, which always has some idea of gaining or achieving something or worse still, of thinking it already knows.

The simple (but not easy) practice of breath-centred meditation requires more effort than lifting weights in the gym or driving a hundred balls on the range. If, however, you can commit – and I hope this book will encourage you to do just that – you are virtually guaranteed, as one of my students said, to be "curiously happier" on the golf course, to hit more sublime and effortless shots, and to win more games.

So let's get to it.

Berkshire, August 2018

PART ONE

THE QUIET MIND

*"The mind is naturally restless and
unsteady Arjuna, and to control it is
as difficult as controlling the wind."*

Bhagavad Gita

UIET MIND

don't really know where thoughts come from or even how to define a thought in biological terms, although evidence supports the claim that they somehow emerge from neural processes within the brain. This neural activity continues to produce thoughts every waking and even every sleeping second: it's a relentless and systemic process that is so habitual it's hardly noticed and even more rarely subdued.

The nature of our thoughts is influenced by everything from random stimuli and circumstances to our own experiential history, yet mostly what's generated are either memories of the past, which see us chew over events long gone, or our fantasies and imagination concerning future scenarios. These thoughts continually interrupt our ability to be quiet, *present* and engaged in the actual moment we're living.

This entire mechanism continues when you're on the golf course: the past mistakes and triumphs taking you away from the present shot, the bad shots you can't seem to let go, your mind racing into the future as you visualise just two more birdies and a par before lifting the trophy. The incessant stream of your own thoughts goes on and on, all the while taking your priceless attention away from the present moment, the only moment in which your mind can be quiet.

Attention. It's a word often bandied around in golf's so-called mental game – specifically voluntary and involuntary, soft or sharp, wide or narrow – in an attempt to explain the various ways in which focusing mental energy can be useful for different aspects of the game such as walking to the tee, setting up to the target or playing your way out of a hazard. I've even written about these things myself and it is all very interesting.

However, most of what we call attention is the scattered mind simply noticing its own thoughts: thoughts that prevent it from being quiet. For instance, your attention is drawn outwards to the line of trees down the right-hand side of the fairway, or it's drawn inwards to a multitude of swing thoughts you're running over in your mind, or it's drawn to the past and the memory of the shot you played on this green the last time you were on this course.

It's very rare for human beings to be in the present moment: we're either daydreaming, listening to our internal dialogue or on autopilot. Yet it seems so many coaches now talk about 'being in the now', and you have to wonder how many of them even pause to take a breath and notice how very far away they are from being *present*.

You see, it's an easy thing to understand intellectually, but it's such a difficult thing to actually do. Mostly the mind likes to think about and talk to itself rather than open up to the direct experience of stillness and with it, the momentary detachment from the relentless cycle of self-talk.

To see the reality of this situation, and the fact that being in the moment requires a particular kind of effort, we need to journey back through centuries-old philosophy and practice to find the essence of humanity's struggle to be *present*. That's what much of this book is about.

In my own journey over the past three decades, training and teaching meditation and Tai Chi, I've been fascinated by the link these ancient arts create between breathing, the quiet mind and fluidity of motion. I've spent the past 18 years exploring this in sport and other performance situations where pressure comes into play.

I've discovered that even motion as complex as the golf swing (the most difficult and complicated of any movement in sport apart from the jump shot in basketball) can become effortless, sublime, powerful and precise, when the golfer (whether a tour professional or weekend hacker) somehow quietens their mind and allows the innate wisdom of their body to perform the shot uninterrupted by analytical thinking, which always includes thoughts of 'getting it right'.

Maybe you've experienced this yourself? The perfect shot. Everybody I've spoken to about this phenomenon tells me it's *effortless* – somehow it just seems to happen. This is the effortless effort of Zen, which we'll talk about as we journey together, along with why, when you try again on the next shot to repeat the previous effortless shot, disaster strikes as you slice or top the ball, ending up off the fairway or in the water. This is one of the paradoxes about performance: the harder you try, the worse it gets.

Training the attention on the breath is the simplest, most direct way to experience both the present moment and the effortless golf shot. By following the natural physical process of breathing, you unite the mind with the body and allow movement to flow. Only the quiet mind can hold our attention where we are. Only by placing our attention where we are can we quieten the mind. By itself the mind cannot be silent, but training the mind for stillness by using the breath is possible when effort is made in this regard.

Some call this the meditative state or Zen-mind. It's also been identified as the zone or flow. It is the ideal state from which to overcome first tee nerves and drive with distance and accuracy down the fairway. It is also the ideal state from which to chip with finesse or one-putt to victory. The trouble is, while the process is simple, in that your mind and body perform in sync when you pay attention to your breathing and get out of your own way, it's not easy. If it were easy, every golfer would be shooting in the 70s every time they stepped on to the course.

The deliberate act of focusing on the breathing is a centuries-old practice dating back over 2,500 years to the Buddha. It's a simple process of sitting quietly, paying attention to the breath, but what a struggle it is, especially as the mind can easily imagine it is meditating and can fantasise or contemplate and intellectually understand the benefits of the practice while talking to itself the whole time you're sitting on your chair or cushion.

Meditation is not contemplation. It is not listening to New Age music or a guided imagery journey on your smartphone app. That's called zoning out. At the very best it's a beginner's entry level attempt or simply a way of unplugging from the cacophony of external and internal noise in the endeavour to find stillness. However, it requires very little in the way of self-enquiry or effort, and without effort, nothing can be achieved.

The quiet mind can be accessed only through the discipline of striving to quieten it, first by seeing how noisy and unrelenting the internal dialogue actually is and then by moving the attention to the breathing and undertaking the age-old struggle of continually bringing the attention back to the breath each and every time it wanders.

At the centre of it all, amid all the thoughts that circle ever around, is a quiet place that belongs only to you. If you've never been there, haven't visited it for a while or would like to go more often, now is the time to begin.

Imagine your attention as a candle flame flickering in a draft from an open window: focusing on the breath in meditation is like closing the window (of your mind), thus reducing the draft (incessant mental chatter) and allowing the flame (attention) to burn more brightly and steadily.

Strengthening the attention, having it unite with your breathing so that your mental energy follows the physical sensation of inhaling and exhaling, transports you to that quiet place from where you will perform your best shots on the golf course. It can also have a transformative effect on your life.

So many of my students speak to me about the joy of golf, the joy of the surroundings, the joy of being outdoors in nature, the joy of the perfect shot, but this can be experienced only by staying with each breath, each shot, each hole – one at a time.

But that's easier said than done. And you mustn't try too hard.

RELAXED CONCENTRATION

The meditative state is one of relaxed concentration, quite unlike any other internal condition available, and it begins to be accessible only once your mind is quiet. It's the experience of being *present*, 'in the zone' or flow state (to use sporting terms), where the focus of your attention is on the task at hand (holing out on the 18th) but you're not thinking too much or trying too hard. How can we quantify this?

Relaxation and concentration are two seemingly opposing forces, which ordinarily don't coexist, but which are necessary for effortless movement to occur, particularly when you're under pressure to make the shot.

Something special lies in the meeting of these two states and it can be trained only via breath-centred meditation: it's not a mental game 'technique' like motivational thinking, goal setting or neurolinguistic programming, but a deep and purposeful practice.

When you're focused but relaxed you're paying attention in the moment and are still aware of what's going on around you, especially the environment and the beauty of the natural world, which, if you can open up to it, can contribute enormously to the internal state you're looking for.

It also activates the occipital lobe at the back of the brain, slowing down the brainwaves and allowing for increased visual acuity and greater perception – remember when Tiger Woods could stop mid-swing if there was a fly on the ball? Those were the days when Tiger was in the zone.

On the golf course, most players over-focus and try too hard, using an inordinate amount of mental energy (interference) thinking about the technical and mechanical aspects of the swing, such that they are no longer even *present*, enjoying some of the most glorious locations on Earth. Instead they disappear into the minutiae of their minds.

When you are thinking about moving you're engaging the prefrontal cortex (PFC), the newest (in evolutionary terms) part of our brains, which governs thinking processes like comparison, understanding and analysis. You may rightly have used this part of your mind all day at work and most likely during a lesson with your swing coach and on the driving range afterwards as you attempt to hone the new learning.

Using this part of the mind to try and control the complex motion of your golf swing during play spells complete game disaster as it interrupts the signal destined for the motor system (the part of the brain responsible for movement), disrupting the chain of events in your neurons, muscles and tendons, all of which can fire quite happily in the right sequence without you interfering.

So it's not the ordinary everyday mind that's required on the golf course, but something else, a state in which you are attentive and yet relaxed. Perhaps this state is already there, underneath the mental chatter and noise you've got used to?

Research shows that the zone or flow state experienced by golfers, especially around the greens, is akin to the Zen-mind achieved by regular practitioners of meditation – the simple (but not easy) art of focusing on the breath.

When you're in the zone (or in deep meditation), there is an experience of inner quiet and a pulling away or detachment from distractions both internal (difficult emotions, memories, adding to your to-do list) and external (traffic noise, television, children playing).

The PFC goes offline or shuts down altogether with regular practice, allowing for a more unified experience of self, one where the mind is quiet, the body is relaxed and the emotions are kept in balance.

You can't think your way into a state of relaxed concentration: it can be activated only through the process of meditation, which is the honing of your focus of attention on the simplest, most fundamental action that's keeping you alive and able to play golf – your breathing.

If you're uncomfortable about the word 'meditation' and its religious or spiritual connotations, don't be! Many people mistakenly believe Buddhism (the wellspring of Zen) is a religion, when it's actually more like a practice: you cannot really 'be a Buddhist' but you can practice Buddhism – the detachment from the mind and negative emotions, through your daily effort of meditation.

A little reverence wouldn't hurt, however, otherwise it's like saying you can exist quite happily without your breathing or that somehow you know better than the divine intelligence that gave you life and can harmonise the complex mechanisms of your mind and body and arrange for them to work together perfectly for the 1.5 seconds of the average golf swing.

All the problems you have on the golf course stem from not trusting this innate intelligence that lives within you and of which you are a part. Trying to control it, organise and interfere with it, thinking that you know and can do better, is the road to golfing misery.

Studies on Zen-mind or the meditative state of relaxed concentration show two vitally important changes of perception, which are phenomenally useful for your golf game.

When you focus on and follow your breathing you greatly reduce the internal dialogue, such that you have fewer thoughts about yourself, your performance and the score. This allows you to play each shot as it happens and not dwell on past holes or project your mind into the back nine.

You stop talking to yourself about outside distractions too: these can be anything from the weather, overly chatty companions or fellow players trying to give you advice on your grip. You also won't be rushed, but will feel you have all the time in the world to make the shot. This is one of the main indicators of being in the zone.

One breath at a time, one shot at a time, one hole at a time.

Relaxed concentration is not a mental game, tip or trick. You can't manufacture it or force it into being through an effort of mental willpower, nor is it a psychological technique that you can call upon without doing the necessary work to cultivate this state through your daily practice.

Again, it's a practice and not a 'technique'.

It can be achieved only through effort, but not an effort of willpower, that is, you can't force it any more than you can make yourself get in the zone. All you can do is make effort towards passivity, effort towards getting out of your own way, effort to quieten the mind, effort to follow the breath and by doing so you allow a change in your internal state.

If you train yourself in this way, with time given each day to sitting quietly, following your breathing with your attention, you can recall it on the golf course when you feel anxious, nervous, uptight or excited or to refocus when it's your turn to putt for the championship.

It's interesting to note that as more technical books have been written about the golf swing and the more golfers fill their heads with mechanical details, the worse people are playing. A symptom of western culture per se, and the golf industry as a microcosm of this wider trend, is that we're suffering from acute collective attention deficit hyperactivity disorder (ADHD) as our minds have become overly obsessed with information now on-tap 24/7 at the push of a button (or the swipe of a screen).

So you will need to keep working to find this coveted state of relaxed concentration because the pull back into the non-focused, scattered mind with its untrained attention going hither and yon is just too great to overcome without consistent training: this default setting has become the natural tendency of the western mind and you must struggle to resist it if you want to play effortless golf.

The practice of sitting quietly, training the attention to follow the breath that comes and goes from your body naturally, peacefully and without any effort on your part is the way to experience more joy, happiness and inner peace, as well as more birdies and golf trophies.

REDUCING SELF-INTERFERENCE

Or: "If I could only get out of my own way!"

Your brain, body and nervous system have an innate intelligence that has formed over eons and is connected with the vast intelligence of the greater cosmos; this can function quite happily without you making an appearance and interfering like an annoying flatmate.

In fact, the optimal functioning of all the thinking, feeling and moving parts of your being while you're playing golf requires only that you get out of the way. Easier said than done!

However, there is a formula that might help; it's taken from the groundbreaking work of Mihaly Csikszentmihalyi, the Hungarian psychologist and author of *Flow: The Psychology of Optimal Experience*, and Timothy Gallwey, the *Inner Game* pioneer and author.

In order to play golf in a state of relaxed concentration, the following three things are necessary:

Skill plus **passion** minus **mental interference**

Research shows that technical **skill** plateaus after about three years of learning, at which point the average person stops improving. What's required after this time is not what the consensus reality of the golf industry would have you believe: further development as a golfer is not dependent on learning ever-more about swing mechanics and buying the latest driver.

Most players' games flatline after about three years and they stay more or less where they are, instead of getting better.

Counter-intuitive as it may seem, after the three-year marker, the more you continue to learn and take on board mentally about swing mechanics and so forth, the more likely you are to see your game deteriorate and your handicap increase. Even more alarmingly, you could be like many lost golfers who come to me in one last desperate attempt, after almost giving up the game entirely in complete frustration.

It's interesting to note that as human beings we each have the capability to block our potential (with self-interference) as well as to free ourselves from the destructive effects of the over-analytical mind (using breathing awareness).

Observing yourself in this regard, and seeing your tendency to interfere and try too hard, is far more important than learning ever more about spine angles, swing planes and geometry.

A fundamental grasp of swing mechanics is necessary, of course, but what I'm saying and what research shows is that after three years it becomes counterproductive and a hindrance to your development as a player to fill your head with ever more technical information which will serve only to interfere with your body's ability to produce a natural and effortless shot.

Moreover, if your mind is not quiet at address, then the mind and body cannot unite, but will work against each other as your thoughts (knowledge and information) try to control and organise your swing (complex motion) instead of letting your body move freely (flow), which can only result in clumsy and ineffective movement.

If skill plateaus after three years, then what of **passion**, the second requirement in the formula for playing golf in the zone?

I like to think of martial arts pioneer and philosopher Bruce Lee's instruction on 'emotional content', which is subtly different from being emotional. As in kung fu sparring, you can never play golf well in an excited state, especially when negative emotions like anger or fear are aroused.

Instead it's important that your passion for the game is kept in check on the course and that your emotions (even so-called positive emotions like excitement) are contained.

Keeping a balance between your mind, your body and your emotions is crucial for maintaining internal equilibrium and enjoying fluidity of movement. Focusing on your breathing is the only way to quieten your mind and develop a calm and neutral mood state; we'll continue to explore why this is so as we journey through the book.

The final and most essential part of the equation – minus **mental interference** – means above all that this equilibrium must be activated so that you get out of your own way *before* taking the shot.

Analysis paralysis, the anathema to fluid motion, comes about when the attention is scattered rather than unified at address, even if part of your mental energy is focused on so-called mental game techniques.

You'll know this first-hand if you've ever set up to the ball with half a dozen or more swing thoughts in your mind, while fixating on your grip, looking to the target and trying to visualise the shot, simultaneously reframing your thinking about the last time you played this hole. Second-guessing yourself by constantly looking at the hole on the green is another example of the mind taking precedence and unbalancing the harmony between thinking, feeling and moving.

Known as 'monkey mind' in the East, scattered attention sabotages, interferes with and undermines your best attempts at effortless movement, as it cannot stay in the present moment and assist in the unification between mind and body.

This has been coined the 'inner chimp' by sports and business coaches using a model of the brain that involves a human, a chimp and a computer – the suggestion being that you use another part of your mind to train the chimp, which perhaps misses the point.

While this might be great for managing thinking in business or to some extent when preparing to compete, it will not help you produce effortless motion when you're out on the 18th green under pressure to produce the winning putt.

You cannot solve mental game issues with more thinking or even with different ways of thinking, especially in golf and other sports. While you may have some success in the short term, it will not be long-lasting as the mind always goes back to the patterns it knows and is comfortable with.

This is why techniques such as drawing a red dot on your glove to help you focus or stepping over an imaginary blue line after taking your shot to help let it go, need changing frequently. These mental game constructs simply fade into the background as your mind stops seeing and reacting to them.

So what's the solution? You guessed it, breathing awareness – the one and only thing that can establish you firmly in the present moment, again and again and again.

The legendary Tom Watson, winner of eight Major tournaments (a US Open title, two Masters, and five Open Championship victories), said that when he learned how to breathe he learned how to win.

Reducing self-interference (the third part of the equation) by getting out of your own way is the most important thing you can do to allow yourself to perform under pressure and win, but you can't train this ability with more thinking, psychological techniques or mental game tips.

You can, however, train it with the regular practice of meditation, which encourages the scattered and wandering monkey mind to be subdued and your attention to be unified such that you reduce the default tendency towards over-thinking technique and trying too hard to make the shot.

If your monkey mind can be occupied with something other than thinking, ie focusing on and following your breathing, it alters the brainwaves, reduces analysis and shuts down the overly active PFC, allowing access to the now. When you are *present* in this way over the ball you are more relaxed, your muscles are more pliable and your mind and body can work together.

Having put aside the intellect and the excessive use of mental energy in an attempt to 'get it right' and having neutralised the emotions so that you're calm and in balance, you allow the innate wisdom of the mind-body connection to manifest. These internal conditions create the potential for you to deliver the perfect shot.

This book is about training those internal conditions, which are imperative to have in place before movement begins. It's simple, but not easy, as it requires letting go of the things you're perhaps most attached to, such as all your knowledge about swing mechanics – even though the more you know the more in your own way you can get.

Knowledge of geometry, physics, angles and swing plane are all very interesting and you can spend hours on the range tweaking and tinkering, but when you start your walk to the first tee you must put all these things aside, along with all the mental game tips you might have read.

Standing at address, there is only one place your mind must be to ensure you drive off with the distance and accuracy you're so capable of delivering – and that's in the present moment.

BEING IN THE PRESENT

Being in the present moment is almost impossible for the average person and extremely difficult even for those who are wont to try. As we've already seen, the mind is constantly restless and drawn away from being in the now by our wandering attention, which is continually flitting from one internal preoccupation to another, as well as responding to outside influences and filtering out background noise –things often occurring all at the same time.

Psychologists have estimated that the experience of being *present* ('Me, Here, Now.') lasts approximately 12 seconds. That figure is quite alarming and holds true even for experienced meditators, as it suggests we can *be where we are* for no more than two or three breaths before the attention starts to wander.

A colleague recently suggested that the term 'being in the now' is so overused in popular culture that it has become nothing more than a trite cliché. Something is surely rotten in the state of the world when a practice as deep and purposeful as the attempt to be *present* pales into insignificance, lost in the mire of the endless data stream coming at us day and night.

Making this effort serves a far higher call than simply winning your next golf game, but it will most definitely stand you in good stead for creating the internal conditions necessary for hitting an effortless golf shot. It may also help you to understand that there is something else beyond the ego that comes into play when the perfect shot manifests itself. Perhaps you've felt this already, that there's something other-worldly about being in the zone.

But how do you begin or progress on this most profound of all journeys?

Seeing how far away your mind and attention are from being in the present is often the first stage in this process. There is value in witnessing the cacophony of ceaseless noise inside your mind and admitting how much it pulls you one way and then the next, into the outside world of distractions or towards your inner world of hopes, memories and imaginary fears.

An inability to sit quietly following your breathing for even two or three minutes and a resistance to the very quiet your mind most needs are also valuable experiences, as on this path what you find most difficult is often what is most needed.

Witnessing your wandering mind during play is also helpful.

This might mean seeing how you berate yourself for the poor shot you've just played, ruminating about it while walking to the next ball and, worse still, how you keep this negative internal monologue going over several more holes or even over the next couple of days.

It also means seeing how you so easily fall into the trap of projecting your mind into the back nine and thinking about the score you may need.

Neither of these scenarios is helpful in quietening your thoughts and delivering fluid motion, as your mind and therefore your attention will be either in the past or in the future, rather than in the present moment.

It's a sorry state of affairs for humanity that everyone is elsewhere for 99% of their day, caught up in the default autopilot setting of habitual thoughts, emotions and behaviour. However, without wishing to appear flippant, the 12-second 'Zen-mind' window, the only barometer against which to measure how *present* you can be, is perfect for your golf game.

What if you could find it within yourself to make a commitment to meditation practice, training regularly, no matter what, and with this increased ability to focus your attention on your breathing, monitor and notice your mood states, quieten your mind, calm your emotions, master your biochemistry, enhance the fluidity of your swing and significantly raise your performance levels?

What do you think your game would look like then?

Focusing on the breath is essentially a form of 'attention training' that keeps you in this moment, this breath, this shot, this hole. It sounds so simple, but of course is anything but, especially when all the mind wants to do is run away with itself.

Mastery over the game is really mastery over yourself and that requires discipline, exploration and self-training, in addition to any swing or performance coaching you may have from outside experts.

Staying in the present moment is the only way to achieve mastery in the game of golf. Jack Nicklaus, the greatest player of all time, talked about self-mastery in his book, *Golf and Life*. Perhaps more than in any other sport, in golf the greatest opponent, perhaps the only opponent you ever really have (apart from the course), is yourself.

Staying in the present moment requires staying close to your breathing and this pull can sometimes be very strong, such as when you're feeling confident, in which case your breath becomes just that little bit deeper and more purposeful. Or the link to your breath can be tenuous, like a thin thread, such as when you're nervous standing over an important shot, thinking too much, letting your chest become tight until you can't even feel your hands grip the putter.

Yet if you pause and take a moment to breathe, the link between the mind and the body can be quickly re-established.

Once you connect with your breathing you will be able to feel your hands, loosen your grip and relax your arms, softening the upper body. This immediately counteracts adrenaline, nerves and excitement, and gets you out of your analytical mind and into your physical body, firmly establishing you in the present moment.

But the trick is to remember you're breathing, which is why the daily practice of meditation is so important.

It's preprogrammed and honed over years of conditioning for you to want to think your way through the shot, engage in self-talk, recalling technical and psychological tips and tricks you've seen and read, before you even realise this is what you're doing, all thanks to the default setting of wandering attention.

Yet the ability to engage with the breath, to slow down and really follow this sensation, encouraging stillness and relaxation *before* you take the shot will pay off a hundredfold in better ball-striking and lower scores.

When the time comes and you're in contention, instead of going into panic mode and awakening the stress response in your nervous system by quick and shallow breathing; instead of feeling nervous, rushing the shot and blowing your chance, you will know how to prepare yourself, keeping your emotions neutral and your biochemistry under control by embracing the stillness before motion, setting up the right internal conditions that will allow the shot to go effortlessly from your intention (mind) through the body (movement) to the desired target.

Remember these are just words and it all sounds so easy perhaps that you might kid yourself that you're already there and you've got this. But it's not until you knuckle down and get into your practice that you will really reap the benefits of meditation in your game and life.

Presence requires practice. Being in the present moment on the golf course requires that you've done your daily practice and remembered to come back to your breathing 100 times each day. Otherwise it's a good idea, but it won't help your game.

But does being *present* mean you're aware only of yourself and whatever you're intent on doing? Not really. Even though some very prominent mental game coaches advocate 'getting unconscious' when you're on the green about to make a difficult putt, this is simply zoning out and is not the ideal state to be in the moment or from which to produce effortless movement.

The experience of real presence includes 'Me, Here, Now.' and thereby must include some perception of your surroundings and the experience of yourself within those surroundings.

IMMERSION

Let's look again at the formula for being 'in the zone' but from a slightly different perspective, really examining the words that are used in our search for their deeper meaning.

'Skill plus passion minus mental interference' can also be expressed as follows:

Skill plus **passion** plus **immersion**

The usual way of thinking about immersion is that it's an experience of being totally engrossed in an activity to the exclusion of everything else.

Therefore, the formula could mean that a golfer can access the zone if they have the necessary skill (bearing in mind the three-year plateau), passion (embracing 'emotional content') coupled with a state of immersion in the shot, to the extent that nothing else exists.

But is this really what's required in order to be in the present moment, the only moment it's possible to experience the quiet mind and hence the fluid motion necessary to play effortless golf?

I recently had a conversation about this with another female martial artist, someone like me who's been training for a lifetime, although her path took her towards the Japanese arts of Karate and Aikido, while I embraced the Chinese traditions of Tai Chi and kung fu.

As women who've trained for many decades and who have learned to love the discipline required for this commitment, we've both experienced frustration with students who don't practise. While she developed a school of martial arts under the direction of a Japanese master, I went on to work with sportspeople, who also inherently embrace the rigours of consistent effort and training.

We were discussing the difference between being 'in the zone', ie immersion in a true sense as we understand it through our practice, and simply 'zoning out', which is what most people mistake for the precious experience of relaxed concentration, the meditative state.

For instance, you experience zoning out when you're scrolling through your phone, playing games on your computer, reading the paper or getting lost in a film – this is complete and total absorption, immersion to the extent that you're oblivious to everything around you and disappear into the activity.

In this state you not only forget yourself, but you forget about the very thing that's keeping you alive – the fact that you're breathing.

Zone out in a kung fu fight or while sparring and you're going to get your backside kicked; zone out on the golf course and while you might have some occasional good fortune – the accidental experience of spontaneous excellence resulting in a great shot – without training that vital space between concentration and relaxation by focusing on your breathing, you can't guarantee that you'll understand how the effortless shot manifested itself or indeed how to recreate it.

This lower level of immersion, which entails getting lost in the activity, losing yourself in what you're doing, might feel nice, but as far as the attention goes it's simply laziness, an easy option, and a path of least resistance. It takes you away from your breathing, away from your body and away from the present moment. As such it really cannot take you towards the expression of the perfect golf shot.

When you become immersed in the intricacies of your pre-shot routine – with its sometimes quite elaborate details, including a preparation box and playing box, stepping over an imaginary blue line and so forth, all of which require a tremendous amount of brainwork and mental energy – you are simply engaging the analytical mind (PFC), which encourages shallow breathing and creates feelings of anxiety in the nervous system, causing tension in your muscles, which then hinders your ability to really let your swing flow.

Conversely, when you divide your attention between your breathing and strategising or visualising etc, something altogether quite different occurs. Now part of your attention can remain on your body, on your breath and in the moment instead of being swallowed up by the mind. The experience of relaxed concentration, 'the zone', is thus encouraged to manifest itself, equipoised in the delicate balance between trying and not trying too hard, between thinking and not thinking too much.

So true immersion is an inclusive experience, not one that cancels out yourself or your surroundings, but that consists of and embraces both.

The question is, can you still pay attention to your breathing while you're immersed in the shot; in other words, can you divide your attention between your breathing and what you're doing?

Even though you're breathing all the time, it's a big ask and, as with the ability to be in the present moment, it requires tremendous effort and continual practice.

We'll look at this more deeply in the chapter on Dividing Your Attention (p102); for now, the ancient teaching on self-observation can help us.

Like most truths, this has been watered down to become more palatable and less demanding, working its way into life-coaching scenarios along with motivational thinking and neurolinguistic programming, but its roots lie in the ancient mystery schools of the East, not in psychology.

Self-observation establishes that there is a part of your mind that can observe yourself, seeing that you are standing on the golf course, your hands lightly gripping your 4-iron, breathing deeply, feeling the sun touch your face and your feet upon the earth beneath you as you prepare to take your shot.

This is true immersion, which includes yourself and your surroundings in the picture.

If you can see yourself in this way it raises the assumption that there are different levels of the mind, and a higher, more conscious level, which simply sees, as opposed to the restless monkey that provides a continual background of chatter to accompany your activities.

Imagine a camera following you around on the course, a camera that is detached and dispassionate so that it neither praises you for the good shots nor berates you for the poor shots, but simply plays the part of a casual observer.

This simple attitude of mind will ensure that you don't lose yourself entirely in the minutiae of your pre-shot routine, but retain an overview of yourself, an overarching eye that can begin to see the various mood states that arise and fall over a round. Helping you distance yourself from them (staying neutral) while noticing the fundamental relationship between your breathing, the quiet mind and fluidity of movement.

Being aware of yourself on the golf course also means paying attention to your surroundings, whether it's the ocean or mountains creating a majestic backdrop, or you're simply appreciating a damp autumn morning at your local course with the sun low in the sky and the birds happily twittering and going about their business.

Noticing the beauty of creation can help you stay in the present moment and in flow.

There is a wonderful piece in Michael Murphy's classic book, *Golf in the Kingdom*, where the enigmatic teacher Shivas Irons advises Murphy that:

"The game requires us to join ourselves to the weather, to know the subtle energies that change each day upon the links … It rewards us when we bring them all together, our bodies and our minds … rewards us when we do and treats us badly when we don't."

The kind of soft fascination that nature exerts on us (if we but open our eyes and look around) is an effortless form of attention that can help free up the cognitive mind, allowing the PFC to rest and relax. The mind is still engaged, but somehow is less fatigued, allowing us to remain *present* in our breathing and in the moment.

When you focus on your technique and try too hard to make the shot, becoming oblivious to yourself and nature, there is no space left in which the zone or flow can manifest itself. Again, as Shivas Irons said to Murphy, *"Ye try too hard and ye think too much … let the nothingness into yer shots."*

Unfortunately, the more you know about technique, the more the mind wants to interfere and often the worse you can play, unless of course you can adopt the mindset of a complete beginner.

BEGINNER'S MIND

A beginner often 'knows' very little, but can have a purity of recognition, an insight or instinct that comes from somewhere deeper than the mind.

Often when I was teaching a Tai Chi class, a beginner would come and join us for their first lesson and I could generally learn something from the way they performed a particular movement from the form or from an innocent question they asked.

The trouble with the expert's mind, especially in the game of golf, is the mistaken belief that the more knowledge a player has about the technical side of the game, the better golfer they will be. Most of the time this simply isn't true, especially when that player has to perform under pressure.

I was coaching a young, driven and very dynamic golf professional a few years back, who suffered from acute analysis paralysis, especially in his short game, as he was so keen to learn everything he could about mechanics and technique. He recounted a story to me about the moment he realised how his desire to 'get it right' was beginning to hinder his ability to make even the simplest of shots with any conviction.

While he was practising on the putting green at his club, obsessively checking his grip, reworking his stance, over-reading the undulations on the green and second-guessing his own best instincts, Alex looked up to see a young girl of about nine sinking the ball into the cup every time. Dumbfounded, he asked the girl what she was thinking about to make all those successful putts, to which she innocently replied, "Getting the ball in the hole!"

You might think this was just so-called 'beginner's luck', but consider the fact that the child's pure and simple approach flowed from the wellspring of her beginner's mind – a stark contrast to the overused and spent mind of the young pro whose 'expert' mind was tying him in knots.

Shunryu Suzuki, the Sōtō Zen monk and teacher who helped popularise Zen Buddhism in the United States during the 1950s, and who founded the first Buddhist monastery outside Asia, said, **"In the beginner's mind there are many possibilities; in the expert's mind there are few."**

A beginner's mind is free and open, in practice, exploration and during performance – while an expert's mind is closed and narrow, limited to what it thinks it knows, signalling death to fluidity of movement.

Thinking, and especially excessive thinking, about technique in no way enhances the rhythm of your movement or helps to connect your mind to your body such that your shots will flow freely. In fact, having fixed ideas as well as a mind that's overworked or confused serves only to cancel out any link the mind may have to the body, as it becomes trapped in the circle of its own influence.

The elite players on tour especially seem to suffer from this, as they tend to fall back on their expert knowledge of mechanics and technique when things aren't going so well, for instance, when they've had a run of poor holes or when they're suddenly in contention or expected to win.

This over-reliance on technique and recalling the data stream of known ideas during performance might enable them to make a reasonable shot, but as the mind-body connection is so tenuous and can be gone in a flash of swing thoughts, the movement produced will be clumsy and ineffective and it simply won't flow, increasing the chance of a poor shot.

Worse still for the future of the game, is the effect of overeager adults on the naturally talented youngsters I've met whose purity of movement and potential for greatness is stifled and all but snuffed out by the so-called 'experts' around them, who try to cram their own knowledge into the poor children's heads.

Then there are the seasoned amateurs who've spent a small fortune on lessons, converting their garage or garden shed into a practice area, buying equipment, learning as much as they can, having lessons, reading instructional articles and so forth, but who end up frustrated and in tears as their games get worse and worse.

These are the golfers who come to me completely burned out mentally, tied in knots from relying on the mainstream approach, which mistakenly assumes that other people, that is, experts, know more than they do about their own minds and bodies.

Yes, it's important to have a basic understanding of the golf swing, but then what – is it better to spend your precious attention recalling the minutiae of swing plane angle or practising how to bring your mind and body together as one?

Doing the latter at times when you're feeling the pressure, especially having the trust and the discipline to follow your breathing, nullifies and dispels all those extraneous thoughts manufactured in the prefrontal cortex, interrupting the signal to the motor system and throwing off your rhythm and timing.

Maintaining a closer link to your body allows your ability for natural movement to come to the fore, as the analytical mind is now otherwise engaged.

Again it's about effort, but the effort to pay attention to what's most important of all, your breathing, which has myriad benefits such as relaxing your muscles, lowering your heart rate, quietening your mind, and calming the anxiety that goes with performing under pressure.

Depending on the mind alone is folly. Having preconceived ideas about the swing without linking your mental intent to your body via your breathing is all but worthless when you have to make the shot. No amount of understanding swing mechanics without the ability to witness and unify your scattered state at set-up will help you play the game the way you want to play it.

But how are you going to move away from over-reliance on your mind, and believing that you have to know all about swing mechanics in order to perform at your best?

It's not so much a leap of faith as recognising something in yourself that you can trust, perhaps by recalling the last time you hit it pure, when your mind was quiet, when you had an easy confidence and your swing flowed because you weren't thinking too much about what you were going to do.

When you hit it pure, you got out of your own way and although at the time it might have been the perfect 'accident', this is something you're capable of experiencing again and again as you learn how to breathe, stay in the present moment and bring your mind and body together as one.

PART TWO

MIND-BODY CONNECTION

"Breath is the bridge which connects life to consciousness, which unites your body to your thoughts. Whenever your mind becomes scattered, use your breath as the means to take hold of your mind again."

Thich Nhat Hanh

MIND-BODY CONNECTION

Stop press! Golf is not a mental game!

It's quite a controversial statement, especially considering that many golfers have bought into the premise that positive thinking, outcome visualisation and the reframing of thoughts in their mind can have an impact on their on-course performance.

These interventions do work to a large extent, but the effects are short-lived and cannot do much to halt the biochemical reactions (anxiety and adrenaline) that pressure arouses in the nervous system when standing on the first tee or putting for the championship.

While I absolutely see the value of achievement psychology, positive thinking, and neurolinguistic-programming as tools to motivate, inspire and prepare you before stepping on to the course, when you are actually playing the game, you need to leave these things in the locker room, along with all those swing tips.

I'm not saying anything negative about mental game coaching or, of course, swing coaching. These things are absolutely necessary for the continual improvement of the sport and for our understanding and development of the athlete golfer.

However, from my experience and the feedback I've had from hundreds of players around the world, it seems that during play, and especially under pressure, another level of attention is required – one that's not concerned with the realm of the mind alone.

Here's why.

The mind cannot control movement. In fact, the wrong use of the mind serves only to hinder the flow of motion. But a mind that is connected to the body can and will enable the performance of movement that is fluid, powerful, effortless and precise.

Golf – perhaps more than any other sport, because the margin of error is so critical – is a game where your mind and your body really need to communicate. Golf is a game of mind-body connection.

To play well, your mind and your movement need to be unified, in sync and seamlessly working together to produce the shot you want. And this just doesn't happen most of the time for most golfers using the mainstream approach that separates the mind from the body, the mental game from the swing, golf psychology from technique. It's nobody's fault, just where things are in the industry at the moment.

Counter to this is the work of Karl Morris who, like me, believes that our understanding of the mind-body connection will be the key determinant in how golf performance develops as the current division of coaching into mental game or technical instruction serves only to separate what most needs to be united.

According to Morris, the quality of your performance can be determined largely by the quality of the questions you ask during play. If you control your questions and ask your brain to come up with solutions or answers to challenges facing you, then you will control your attention and, if you control your attention, you will further enhance the right internal state necessary for your best performance to emerge.

One example of a quality question Morris has used with all players, from high-handicappers right up to the elite professionals is, *"What does a good shot look like here?"*

While this question may look deceptively simple, it can be profound, so long as you ask the question on each and every shot you play so that it becomes an anchor point in your routine.

By asking this question you are in effect focusing your mind. You are not trying to 'be positive', but are simply creating a mechanism to control your attention and your focus. You are not even saying that you *will* hit a good shot, thus ramping up the pressure, and you are not trying to fix your swing or 'get it right': you are simply providing more possibilities for your brain and body to work in harmony, to give yourself the best chance of producing the shot you want to make.

Intention is very powerful, sometimes too powerful, but if you can stay focused on your breathing while asking this and other quality questions, you'll make sure intent doesn't spill over into analysis.

This is important, as it will help you generate an idea, feeling or image of the shot that's still connected to the sensation of your physical body, rather than falling prey to the mental gymnastics of going through your technique when you're about to hit the ball.

To reiterate, you can't think your way to the perfect golf shot; this is something that happens only when the controlling influence of the analytical mind is subdued.

The more the mind tries to take control of and organise movement, the more tension arises in the body and the less fluid and accurate your motion.

Indeed, as Fred Shoemaker writes in *Extraordinary Golf*, it's only when a golfer stops trying to fix their swing that breakthroughs can occur in their awareness.

The mind cannot control movement. It's not fast enough to keep up with the tens of thousands of neurons communicating with your slow and fast-twitch muscle fibres and tendons, seamlessly arranging for them all to fire at the right time, in the right sequence to create the correct chain of events that allows for the 1.5 seconds of one of the most complex movements in all of sport.

As soon as you have a predominant idea, such as a very strong swing thought, without linking this mental intent to the equally strong physical sensation of breathing, then the signal about your intended motion gets captured by the analytical part of your mind, which disrupts the timing of the aforementioned chain of events.

The prefrontal cortex, which you use most of the time in your everyday life and work, is designed only to analyse, evaluate and consider information. If you engage the prefrontal cortex before striking the golf ball, then the signal to the motor system (the part of the brain responsible for movement) will be interrupted, if only for a fraction of a second, but it's enough to hinder the flow of motion and create a disappointing outcome.

Remember, the more relaxed you are and the deeper you breathe, the more you can get out of your own way and allow the innate wisdom of the mind and body to work out the best solution for you.

Here are five keys which, in addition to regular meditation practice, will help to keep the analytical mind quiet and allow for better communication between your mind and body so that your swing will flow.

1. Relaxation

Counter-intuitive as it may seem, relaxation is a master key to peak performance, especially in pressure situations. The ability to notice tension when it arises in the body and to let it go before taking the shot is crucial. This is one reason many of the elite players give a loosening shake or waggle before addressing the ball. Step away or shake out if you feel tight.

2. Connecting with nature

Opening your peripheral vision to take in the scenery around you will help you access the flow state of relaxed concentration. Research shows this is the ideal state from which to attempt any complex movement, as it bypasses the analytical mind and allows direct access to the motor system. Standing on the tee looking into the distance while still retaining some awareness of your body and breathing is the best way to activate this state.

3. Slowing down

A prerequisite for the effortless golf shot is the feeling of having more than enough time. When you rush your shot preparation, there is an immediate disconnection from the body and from the 'here and now' as you are overly anticipating the future, that is, getting on with the shot. Slow down by relaxing and connecting with your surroundings.

4. Gratitude

A recent survey I conducted with my students and online community showed that the experience of *joy* is one of the main reasons players love the game. However, many golfers are so obsessed with angles, geometry and swing plane that they hardly pause to consider what a privilege it is to be able to play a game they love in good company and beautiful surroundings. Taking a moment to be grateful and bring the joy into your game could help you shoot more birdies.

5. Singing or humming

Many golfers choose to hum or sing quietly to themselves while setting up and taking the shot. This is a great way to keep the 'monkey mind' happy as it totally bypasses engagement with the analytical mind and helps you feel relaxed. Finding a tune with a 3:1 tempo is especially good for regulating your swing timing in keeping with that of the tour pros who take two or three times as long to reach the top of their backswing as they do to move from the top down through impact.

BRAIN CHEMISTRY AND PERFORMANCE

Maintaining the essential equilibrium of a relaxed yet focused state in times of pressure is the key to winning at golf, whether it's the local club tournament or a major championship.

The performance of every player I've worked with excels or deteriorates during those singular, high-pressure moments such as the final tee shot or the clutch putt for victory, depending on one factor alone: how aware they are of their breathing and whether they can allow the breath to deepen and slow down before taking the shot.

Breathing affects, alters and influences the chemistry of the brain and with it, the mind-body connection. It's the link between your thoughts and movement. No awareness of breathing, no mind-body connection, no unification of mental game and technique.

Alarmingly, research shows that around 95% of people are breathing in a way that is 'biomechanically unsound', which is to say, they're breathing *vertically* (short and shallow breaths into the chest) as opposed to *horizontally* (long, expansive breaths which make full use of the lower lung capacity by expanding the diaphragm).

It's vital that during play, and particularly when standing over those pressure shots, you breathe in a way that reduces anxiety, supports relaxation and enables your muscles to respond to the mental image you have of the shot you want to play.

If you take shallow, vertical breaths (as most people who've had no breathing training are prone to do) you'll feel anxious and won't play to your potential no matter how much you know about golf technique.

Here's why.

The brain is the primary organ affected by anxiety, and it's also the primary organ that influences movement. When anxiety centres are aroused in the brain the autonomic nervous system (which regulates the breathing, the heart rate and digestive processes) is activated.

The stress response, which is hardwired into our nervous systems and manifests itself when we feel under threat, is automatically triggered and is coupled with quick and shallow breathing into the upper chest. This creates a descending spiral, which no amount of technical or psychological know-how can alter, as the shallow breathing and feelings of anxiety simply compound each other.

The worst case scenario of course is the yips.

However, studies show that deep abdominal (*horizontal*) breathing can change the chemistry of the brain and body by activating the relaxation response in the parasympathetic nervous system, allowing it to take precedence over the feelings of stress and the release of adrenaline, so that we calm down and regain a state of equilibrium.

Let's take a look at a typical pressure situation on the golf course, exploring the relationship between the breathing and the ability to make a winning shot.

To begin with, let's see what happens without paying attention to the breath.

You're one up on the 18th hole and approaching a difficult shot with a bad lie after a hooked drive off the tee and the ensuing pressure immediately and unconsciously triggers the tendency to shallow breathe, thus activating the stress response.

The resulting changes in your body will go something like this.

First your chest will get a little tighter, less oxygen is fed to your brain, your nervous system becomes flooded with adrenaline, your heart beats faster, your muscles shorten and tighten, and this makes your whole body tense.

Feeling tense, you start to over-think technique in an attempt to regain confidence; but you're also likely to rush your pre-shot routine and shorten your backswing, leading to a potentially duff second shot, which will only increase your sense of anxiety, ensuring you keep on with the shallow breathing and thus continue with the ever-decreasing circle of your performance. I call it the **circle of deterioration**.

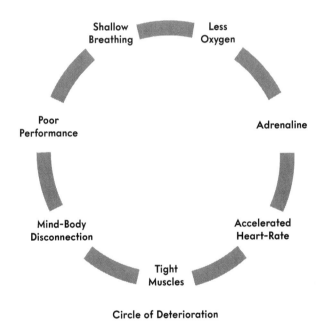

Shallow Breathing

Less Oxygen

Adrenaline

Poor Performance

Accelerated Heart-Rate

Mind-Body Disconnection

Tight Muscles

Circle of Deterioration

Now here's what happens when you take control of your breathing.

You're one up on the 18th hole and approaching a difficult shot with a bad lie after a hooked drive off the tee and the ensuing pressure immediately and unconsciously triggers the tendency to shallow breathe, thus activating the stress response.

However, this time, as you've been practising meditation (you'll soon learn how in Part Three: The Training) you can remember to focus on your breathing and are confident that you know how to expand and deepen the breath and use it to encourage a quiet mind, focused relaxation and fluidity of movement.

Now, instead of allowing your innate stress response to take over and rule your brain, body and nervous system when you're under pressure to perform, you can take conscious control of your state via your breathing, bring your mind and body together and produce an effortless golf shot.

Deep breathing in turn will send more oxygen to your brain, which can flood your nervous system with endorphins, lower your heart rate, relax your muscles, strengthen your mind-body connection, raise your confidence levels, and create a calm yet focused state from which to set up and swing. Physiologists call it the relaxation response; I call it the **circle of excellence**.

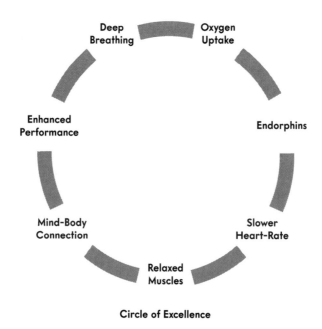

Circle of Excellence

You play golf because you want to win. Of course, you want to enjoy yourself and know that you're improving and playing to a personal standard that gives you satisfaction... but most of all you want to win games, right?

It's been said that in the history of the sport, every game comes down to seconds and inches, even millimetres sometimes. However long you've played, however many lessons you've had, however many hours you've worked on the range, however much you've read and might know about technique, in the end it's all about the way you manage your internal state when the next shot is all that counts and where the outcome either way is all that separates you from victory or defeat.

Learning to love these moments instead of dreading them, learning to engage your competitive spirit instead of getting in your own way, learning to make room for confidence instead of fearing failure, really can be as simple as training awareness of your breathing.

But can you discipline yourself enough to bypass your ingrained habits and create the necessary space to come into your breathing before each shot? As an idea it's fairly simple (which is why so many coaches are touting this nowadays) but in reality it's not that easy – hence the necessity for regular practice, using the ancient daily discipline of concentrating on the breath.

This book is about developing that practice, training awareness of the breath through meditation, thereby encouraging a sensory feedback loop that syncs your mind with your body – a state which you alone have the potential to activate when you're standing over the ball.

SENSORY FEEDBACK LOOP

Mental game techniques and sports psychology are useful preparations before competing, but they can be limited in their effectiveness during actual performance as they stay within the realm of the mind. As you're beginning to see, the only way the mind can have a positive influence on the body and therefore movement, is if it gets out of the way.

You can't think your way to the perfect golf shot: you have to feel and move your way to it with a mind that is connected to the body rather than imprisoned in its own sphere. Let's have a deeper look at why awareness of breathing is the simplest, most direct route to accomplishing this and activating the mind-body connection.

Awareness of breathing, following the breath in meditation practice, creates a sensory feedback loop between your attention (mind) and your breathing (body) and so conjoins thinking with feeling, uniting your mental state with the motion of your swing.

When your mind follows your breathing, you're engaging a mental process with a physical act or sensation; this immediately brings about a connection between thought and movement. It also has the effect of reducing the usually incessant mental chatter as well as nullifying anxiety.

If you can stay with this practice for a period of time each day, and start to check in with yourself, remembering your breathing at regular intervals as you go about your daily life, you will develop this feedback loop, a type of perception or awareness such that you will begin to notice how often you forget all about your body and your breathing and become stuck in your mind.

This will be invaluable training for your golf performance as noticing when you're out of sync, over-thinking, rushing, gripping the putter too tightly, feeling anxious on the tee and so on, will act as a reminder to follow your breath and help you get back into flow before taking the shot. Seeing how often you forget to remember your breathing is also priceless training.

Equally important is to discover and experience the different mood states that are created depending on where you breathe from. Most people shallow-breathe into the upper chest most of the time throughout the day, which means that the stress response is continually being activated and a background anxiety or uptightness is apparent even during the most relaxing of activities. If you take this on to the golf course, you can kiss goodbye to winning ever.

Relaxing the chest and inhaling into the lower abdomen is the most natural way to breathe, and is how we breathed as children before the ego developed and we started to become self-conscious. Filling your lungs from the bottom with deep, horizontal breaths that open up the diaphragm activates the relaxation response which can help us to feel calm and centred, even in the most difficult of situations.

Don't get caught up with holding the breath for a certain count, or alternately breathing through the nostrils and the mouth, or any other elaborate teachings on breath control; they won't serve you well on the golf course. This is a simple practice, a deep practice and not a technique.

Your training is all about awareness – are you aware that you're breathing or are you lost in your mind or caught up in your emotions?

When you come away from your breathing, you're coming away from the present moment and with it the mind-body connection, the coveted state of unification that above all else allows for fluid, effortless and precise movement.

You've doubtless seen time and again during golf games how you ruminate about poor shots played over the previous holes and how you project yourself into future holes by imagining the pars or birdies you've yet to make.

Have you noticed though, that when your mind gets busy, your breath gets quicker and shallower and you come away from being 'in the now'? Even so, you still set up to the shot in this condition, which creates all kinds of problems with the motion of your body – and then of course you try to fix this by learning more about swing mechanics.

With your daily meditation practice you'll begin to see this and moreover, you'll know exactly how to bring yourself back to the present moment by working your breathing before addressing the ball.

For instance, when approaching and stepping on to the greens, many golfers, even the tour pros, get uptight and nervous. Remember the circle of deterioration? Well, contrary to popular myth, the first thing to break down when your short game falls apart is not your technique but your breathing, which then creates feelings of anxiety in the nervous system, arousing mental interference and disrupting the mind-body connection.

This usually manifests itself in the following way.

As the breath becomes shallow (you might even hold your breath over the putt), the energy rises into the upper chest and head, you're no longer in your feet or your hands (your grip pressure has likely got tighter) and you start over-thinking, looking at the hole too much, second-guessing yourself, being hesitant. Or the opposite might happen and you'll rush everything from your shot preparation to taking the putter back as your movements match your internal rhythm of a faster heart rate and quicker breaths.

Taking just a few moments to become aware of the involuntary, preprogrammed effects of the stress response and redirecting the breath so that it becomes deeper and slower before you begin your shot preparation can seem like an enormous undertaking as you have to override aeons of conditioning hardwired into the human nervous system.

It's also a massive paradigm shift you've got to get your head around, but if you can trust the research, trust the process and trust yourself – if you will only slow down a little, notice when you've come away from the present moment and with it your breathing and then rework the sensory feedback loop to activate the relaxation response – you'll hole that putt and make that birdie in a way that will feel joyful and effortless.

Getting underneath the ego, seeing how habituated your reflexes are and knowing how to counter them, gives you less chance of being deflated on the course. Your strength will come from a quiet confidence born of consistent daily effort, giving you the ability to self-regulate and create the right internal conditions (deep breathing, quiet mind, relaxed concentration) before each and every shot.

Can you see why training your breathing is more important than knowing the minutiae of golf swing mechanics?

It's a very humbling thing to admit that the years of effort you've probably put into your game have for the most part been misdirected. It's not that your mind needs to hold more information about spine angles and swing plane, but that it needs to follow your breathing and so conjoin with your body.

A lot more effort is required on this path, but the rewards are well worth it.

In order to experience what can be accomplished in the meditative state, so akin to the zone or flow, you first have to train it and that means daily, so you can learn to direct your attention and your thoughts towards what you intend rather than where your default mental chatter takes you.

Practising getting back in flow when you drop out of it, recalling this state when you're under pressure and seeing how often you let your mind take you away from the now, all require vigilance and consistent effort – as does starting over with your meditation practice the next day and the next and the next.

Zen master Shunryu Suzuki suggests that we **"Follow the breath with a warm-hearted mind"** as this helps bring positive feelings to the practice rather than it being too austere, so try to be gentle and compassionate with yourself (without wimping out on your daily practice!)

But this training, like no other, can open the doorway into greatness on the golf course, as you will know how to create the perfect internal environment from which you can execute more effortless shots.

THE ALPHA STATE

In your meditation practice you may become aware of how when your thoughts become quiet your attention seems to move to the back of your head, to the region known as the occipital lobe.

This is the area where alpha brainwaves are generated, and these waves are the electro-magnetic pulse or rhythm responsible for creating the coveted state of relaxed concentration known as 'the zone'.

Brainwaves are produced by electrical impulses that move between synapses inside the brain.

When you are actively awake, you are typically in a state known as beta, with brainwave activity at a bandwidth of between 14 and 30 cycles per second. When electroencephalograms (EEGs) show a brainwave pattern of 9 to 12 cycles per second, the subject is said to be in the alpha state, usually described as relaxed, peaceful or floating.

It is what scientists associate with 'right-brain' activity, governing the subjective realms of our imagination, creativity and intuition. Edison, Einstein and many other brilliant thinkers considered a daily ritual of accessing an alpha state of mind essential to their work, as it allowed them to be more creative and find solutions to some of the most challenging problems.

When Tiger Woods was at the height of his golfing prowess, he remarked that his creative thinking was his biggest weapon on the course.

We access the alpha state unconsciously in daydreaming and light sleep, but how much better to access it consciously with meditation, so that you can recall this state, almost at will, when you're out on the golf course and need to make the shot.

To play the shot 'in the zone', which you now know is akin to the meditative state, the left hemisphere of the brain (logical thinking) needs to become quiet and the right hemisphere (intuitive thinking) needs to become slightly more active. When this happens, your brain produces more alpha waves, your focus is clearer and yet you are much more relaxed.

Seen in this context, it's obvious why too many swing thoughts (a left-brain activity) nullifies fluid motion. Indeed, the fluidity of your swing, chipping and putting will always be dependent on the strength of your mind-body connection and not on how much you know about technique.

This means that the parts of your brain responsible for movement need to take precedence over those parts responsible for logical and analytical thinking.

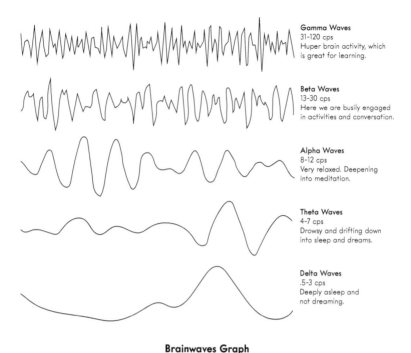

Gamma Waves
31-120 cps
Huper brain activity, which
is great for learning.

Beta Waves
13-30 cps
Here we are busily engaged
in activities and conversation.

Alpha Waves
8-12 cps
Very relaxed. Deepening
into meditation.

Theta Waves
4-7 cps
Drowsy and drifting down
into sleep and dreams.

Delta Waves
.5-3 cps
Deeply asleep and
not dreaming.

Brainwaves Graph

With meditation practice, the brain fundamentally rewires itself. The amygdala shrinks and with it feelings of fear and anxiety; the brain-hemispheres unite, the analytical mind (prefrontal cortex) goes offline and the brain's motor system takes charge of motion, rhythm and timing instead of being interrupted by you trying to get it right.

All you have to do is master your breathing: that means training yourself to remember it, allowing it to deepen and slow down and focusing your attention on your breathing as you set up to the ball. It sounds easy enough, doesn't it?

Yet the zone or flow is available only through deep practice and is not a psychological technique, even though many people still seem to believe it's something you can achieve through an intellectual understanding or by attending a weekend course in mindfulness.

This is really missing the point.

The zone, also known as the meditative state, is an experience beyond the ordinary mind, as anyone who has ever been there in their practice or on the golf course will verify. It is a subtle, elusive and almost other-worldly state, which some have even described as a spiritual experience.

It has nothing to do with achieving a so-called trance-like or unconscious state, which are terms often incorrectly associated with the zone; this is an assumption based on intellectual understanding and not one born of the effort of daily practice.

The thing that's going to make the difference for you on the golf course, especially in those high-pressure moments, is the deliberate and correct focusing of the attention on your breathing – and this takes practice. You might say this practice is the price of freedom on the course; it's the effort needed for golf to become effortless.

Without this training you can still make the shot but as one of my students remarked, it will simply be "forcing the ball down the fairway".

By getting out of your own way, focusing on your breathing and quietening the mind, the brain-body connection can take charge of complex motion, your fast-twitch muscles fire in the right sequence and fluid motion emerges from a calmer, more collected internal state.

Many things can be accomplished in the alpha state.

We know from research that the players with the most successful short games, especially those that continually one- or two-putt on the greens, are generally in the alpha state. So too for those with the subtlety and finesse to play delicate chip shots, which are all about feel and sensing as well as controlling adrenaline.

Course management, better decision-making and the ability to ignore external distractions are other signs of being in the alpha state, but perhaps the most useful skill available is the enhanced capacity to visualise.

Visualisation always works better when your mind is quiet, but many golfers try to incorporate this mental game factor on top of a mind already full of swing thoughts.

In the alpha state, your mind is equipoised between focusing and relaxing and is therefore in the ideal state for you to see your shot before you swing. Moreover, as your mind and body get more in sync with your training, the motion of your swing will match the picture in your head.

TRY THIS:

- As you take a few practice swings, visualise the shot you want to make, starting with the outcome first (just as the great Jack Nicklaus did for all his Major wins). See the ball sitting high up on the green or plum in the middle of the fairway. Next, see the arc of the ball as it flies through the air and then finally, get a clear picture of the swing you need to make, in order to get the results you've just imagined.

- Since your nervous system cannot tell the difference between reality and imagination, this is a great way to train your mind for success on the course, as the more you can envisage yourself making some great shots, the more likely you are to recreate these experiences while actually playing.

- Most importantly, by remembering to focus on your breathing while visualising, you will be more relaxed and this will help you to swing with fluidity and ease.

FLUID MOTION

The secret to fluid motion lies in the moments *before* you start moving.

Just as the zone or flow state is a delicate balance between relaxation and focus, so fluid motion is an exact physical condition poised between holding just the right amount of tension and letting go.

An active relaxation is required from both your body and your mind – in unification – and this can be accessed only by working with your breathing.

To move with fluidity and effortlessness, especially through a sequence of movements as complex as the golf swing, there needs to be some internal stillness, almost like a silent operator working the controls of the perhaps unfortunately named *Golfing Machine* (to quote Homer Kelley's 1979 book, subtitled *The Computer Age Approach to Golfing Perfection*).

It always makes me smile, as I can't help but think about Murphy's law (originally attributed to Major Edward A Murphy, who worked as an engineer in the United States Air Force in the 1940s and 1950s) which states that if something can go wrong with the moving parts of a machine, it will go wrong. But oh how the golf industry loves to have you tinker around with the nuts and bolts, levers and angles, geometry and plane of your swing, not just in practice but while you're actually playing.

The relationship between stillness and motion cannot be overstated, but it cannot even be conceived or approached without consistent training to quieten the mind.

Every golf shot begins from stillness, yet time and again I hear how a player's problems all stem from this gap before taking the shot (in contrast to a game like tennis, where you're reacting to a moving ball). It is seen as a stumbling block to performance rather than something to be embraced.

The mistaken belief is that the pause before movement begins is a time to be filled by going over swing mechanics in your head rather than a time to be quiet and connect your mind to your body by working with your breathing. Yet once you understand the laws of motion as they apply to human performance, you can use the gap before movement to your advantage.

The golf swing is not something to 'get right'. It is not a static movement nor is it a pattern that you can repeat with exactitude, replicating the same thing over and over.

Every game is different, every shot is different; even if you played the same course at the same time every single day of the year there would be different weather conditions, the shots you'd attempt would vary, the lie of the ball would change given the differing undulations on the greens, your own thoughts and feelings would alter, the light on the fairways would fluctuate depending on the season and the angle of the sun in the sky – a million different internal and external variations.

Your golf practice time would therefore be better spent on developing correct posture, alignment and a collected state of readiness than on endlessly trying to fathom out how you can control all the moving parts of your swing.

For now, it's important to remember that even the game's greatest player, Jack Nicklaus, had just a single lesson a year from his coach Jack Grout, who would simply go over the basics of the address, grip and finish positions.

This early training of the Golden Bear echoes the approach of some of the most famous warriors of the eastern world; particularly that of Miyamoto Musashi, the unconquerable Samurai swordsman, and Wang Xiangzhai, the legendary Chinese boxer.

Both these masters practised only stance-keeping and maintaining a relaxed but ready attitude in preparation to draw the sword or throw a punch, respectively. Both soundly thrashed (and sometimes killed) any and all opponents, most of whom trained in the traditional way by learning and repeating forms and katas and patterns of movement.

Let's recap on some of the principles governing fluidity of motion.

- The mind and body must work in unison to achieve perfect motion.

- A quiet mind allows the body to move with fluidity, power and effortlessness, and also enhances the performance of accurate and precise motion, especially when under pressure.

- A state of 'relaxed concentration' allows the mind to set the intent for the motion, to which the body then responds.

- The meditative state and 'the zone' are synonymous: the former trains the mind to achieve stillness, the latter is the experience of stillness while in motion.

- The ability to perform under pressure is best achieved by quietening the internal dialogue and controlling the body chemistry; thus activating the 'relaxation response' and preventing the breakdown of technique.

- Awareness of breathing is the simplest and most direct path to reaching and retaining 'the zone' of relaxed concentration, and can also quickly re-establish a neutral state.

- An equipoised mind, balanced between effort and relaxation, allows the chain reaction of muscles in a complex movement to activate in the correct sequence.

- Over-thinking the technical aspects of motion disrupts the signals sent to the motor system, and results in clumsy, ineffective movement and poor outcomes.

Fluidity of motion is always dependent on the strength of the mind-body connection.

The way to achieve this is by learning to breathe consciously, deeply and slowly, and by seeing when you are not doing this and bringing yourself back to the breath again and again. You must do this in your daily practice, in preparing to compete and when actually playing.

Just this one thing is a lifetime's work. Just this one thing will help you master yourself on the golf course, regulate your emotional highs and lows, nullify your mental interference, control anxiety and allow you to produce more effortless shots by knowing how to create the right internal conditions within yourself as you stand over the ball.

Physical tension is always the result of the mind's interference and the ego trying to control movement: the more you think, the more you try to take over and make the swing, chip or putting stroke happen, the less fluid and accurate the shot will be.

Meditation practice will help you to become more aware of tensions in your face and body and help you to notice these things and actively relax at address, giving you more chance to hit it pure and realise your potential as a player.

You will learn to be quiet inside, building a lasting reservoir of internal peace and detachment that will not be dependent on your mood, your companions or competitors, the weather conditions or how the front nine went.

Inner stillness can be maintained even during movement. The same level of relaxed focus can be in place as you go through your pre-shot routine, pull your club from the bag, take a few practice swings, visualise the outcome and make the swing for real as you seamlessly connect mind to body and clubhead to ball.

The more slowly, quietly and deeply you breathe, the calmer and more relaxed your nervous system will be. The more your mind and body can work together, the more in the present moment you'll be and the more awareness, visual acuity, creativity, ability to solve problems, handle pressure, regroup, and hole out you'll have at your disposal.

Sounds good, yes?

Yet, it doesn't matter whether you're a high-handicap player, a single-figure competitive amateur or a seasoned professional: in order to play effortless golf, a transformation needs to take place in you before it can manifest itself in your game.

With this in mind, let's begin your training.

PART THREE

THE TRAINING

"I am awake to this breathing that is taking place in me. I am awake to my body. I do not separate them from each other."

Jeanne De Salzmann

CONSCIOUS BREATHING

The aim of this book is to help you understand and develop the relationship between your breathing, the quiet mind and winning golf competitions; training that will help you to bring about a stronger mind-body connection and with it, the ability to perform shots that are fluid yet precise, even when you're under pressure.

Many books, newspaper articles and blogs have been written about using breathing awareness in golf and it's easy to assume that if you have a cognitive understanding of the benefits of breathing and meditation, then you're automatically going to reap the rewards, but nothing could be further from the truth.

Practice is the only discipline that guarantees freedom.

You may have noticed I rarely use the term 'mindfulness' to describe the sort of practice I'm advocating, even though (or most likely because) it's the latest buzzword in sport and business.

Instead I'm going to use the term 'conscious breathing' to denote the fact that you'll be training to become conscious of your breath and, moreover, conscious of yourself breathing. This is something you will have to practise, setting aside the designated time each day.

More often than not our breathing is unconscious. We don't have to think about breathing because it's an automatic function hardwired into the autonomic nervous system – it happens without us, and goes on in spite of us, yet it's the most important of all our daily activities. Without our next intake of breath, our life will be measured in minutes. So why can't we pay attention to it; what else is so important that we forget the very thing that is keeping us alive?

From now on I'd like you to try and pay attention to your breathing as you're reading this. Every time you pick up this book, become aware of your breathing and stay with it for as long as you can.

When you forget, come back to it and try again. I don't want you to stop reading, but just follow your breath as you read the book.

You'll soon see why meditation practice is such an epic struggle and how those who are content with their intellectual understanding without making this effort are just wimping out. As the enigmatic teacher of dancing, GI Gurdjieff (1866-1949), said, **"Without struggle, no progress and no result."**

Conscious breathing is about making the effort to be conscious, becoming awake to yourself and this most fundamental of all your actions in this moment and the next and the next. It helps you stay in the present and detach from the incessant flow of thoughts and feelings that take you into an imagined future or see you ruminating about the past long gone.

This practice was first brought to us 2,500 years ago by Gautama Buddha, who taught his followers to hone their attention by placing it on the breath, thereby quietening the restless mind and detaching from negative emotions.

Following the breath creates an anchor of stability and neutrality, helping you to place less importance on the internal chatter and more attention on the moment you're in. Once you train this ability, your mind will be strong enough to stay with the shot you're taking, which, according to Jack Nicklaus, winner of 18 Majors, is the only shot that matters.

There are myriad reasons why this training is so important for your golf game, not least of which is being able to access the zone or flow in the gap before starting your swing.

Neuroscientists who've been studying the brainwaves of world-class athletes have proven the Tai Chi adage that 'Stillness is the Master of Motion' by showing that the athlete with the quietest mind in the moments before movement begins, always exhibits the most effortless motion, especially during the intense pressure of competition.

In other words, the quality of the mind-body connection in the stillness before movement begins determines the quality of the movement that will be delivered.

When you consciously tune into your breathing, allowing it to slow down so that you are breathing deeply and fully, it allows you to deliberately match the rhythm of your breathing to the tempo of your swing.

Time and again my students – from recreational and competitive amateurs, right up to seasoned professionals as well as lifelong golf coaches – have noticed that the quality of their swing is entirely dependent on the quality of their breathing. This changes everything about the game. It is no longer a game of swing mechanics, but that of how conscious you can be of your breathing while you're playing.

"One breath at a time, one shot at a time, one hole at a time" – it's the only way to stop playing 'search for a swing' and start playing effortless golf and is the reward of effort spent in daily practice.

It's all too easy to hold the breath while you're swinging or to take shallow breaths when you're anxious over a putt. These things will serve only to activate the adrenaline and with it feelings of tightness and negative mental chatter, not to mention the fact that your energy will rise up into the chest and head areas, negating your lower-body stability, no matter how much weight you can squat in the gym.

Perhaps now is a good time to introduce you to your body's centre of gravity, known as the 't'an tien' (dantian) in Tai Chi and other *internal* martial arts.

Located approximately three inches below your navel, this area is essential in breathing correctly for enhanced performance. If you continue with this training, you will eventually learn how the t'an tien is involved in the development of a strong, stable base, the initiation of movement and the release of relaxed physical power.

As you develop your meditation practice and your willingness to go back to your breathing again and again, you'll want to make the breath as deep and purposeful as possible. When your attention is placed on the area around the navel, this has the effect of encouraging the breath to begin in the lower abdomen; conversely, when you try to take a deep breath, you end up causing the shoulders to rise and the chest to expand, which has the opposite effect.

Using the eastern approach to performance enhancement, the mind and body are always trained together; when we train the breath we also hone the attention and quieten the mind, and at the same time we develop more relaxation in the physical body, helping to create better balance and more power.

With conscious breathing, your exhalation will become particularly important for helping you to relax and empty your upper body of tightness and tension; it's the moment you can let go and as we'll see later on, this out-breath will become vital for the transmission of energy and power at impact.

For now it's enough to simply train yourself to follow your breathing during your meditation practice and then as often as you can throughout your day, recalling the breath by cutting into the endless stream of unconscious, mechanical thoughts that revolve constantly alongside the external distractions to rob you of your attention.

Only as you develop this necessary skill and ability to continually come back to the breathing, no matter what else is going on inside or around you, can you then bring it into your game.

If you could just begin to not take the breath for granted; if you could only practise, really commit no matter what, this effort alone would help you on the golf course, especially in times of pressure.

As I've said many times already, this is not a mental game technique but a daily practice that teaches you how to focus your attention so that you can be in the present moment, fully aware of yourself and your surroundings as you stand over the ball with a quiet mind and a relaxed yet focused intent.

It's about making a personal effort, a stand against the default setting of the mind, which wants to wander and do its own thing. Thereby undermining your ability and your self-confidence simply because – untrained – it can't help interfering with the signal about motion, which should pass directly to your motor system rather than getting hijacked by thoughts of a technical nature.

Probably the most difficult thing in the world is to be continually conscious of your breathing, because it's an automatic response deep in the brain; so we'd better get started on your practice.

GETTING STARTED

It's important that you make a start today.

Putting off your training until next week is not the way to begin this process.

Fundamentally it requires effort: forcing yourself to make a start whether you feel like it or not.

We are so used to putting effort into the outside world – achieving targets, going to meetings, making money, doing fitness challenges and working towards project deadlines – that it is daunting (to say the least) to sit for a while with all that stripped away and be left with nothing but yourself for company.

This is not so much a journey towards achieving something (although the ability to play a more effortless game of golf will surely follow) but a journey within.

We are conditioned to wanting instant gratification and instant, or at the very least, visible results. I see my muscles toning up, I see that I am losing weight, I see that my bank balance is increasing, but I cannot see my mind quietening down: I can experience it only if I work towards it with a consistent effort.

But that requires going through many thresholds like irritation, boredom, lack of belief in the process, thinking you're the exception and you don't have to do it, feeling uncomfortable, making excuses, an inability to be quiet, feelings of restlessness or wondering if you're doing it right.

Sometimes the first time sitting in meditation is a revelation; many people feel elated and joyful, and get instant results in their golf game. I've also heard many times from potential students, "This is easy," after sitting with them in a coaching session.

However, it's quite usual that these initial experiences lead nowhere; if it's so easy and my game's all right now (goes the scenario), then why should I bother with the practice? And they don't. Yet this training is the one thing that will make the biggest difference on the golf course: without it, the barrier to elite performance can never be crossed.

Committing to new habits requires you to be patient and honour the journey; so you'll simply have to start today and try again tomorrow and every day thereafter.

The Buddhists have a wonderful saying for the inner process that has led you to even consider you might want to meditate, **"That which you are seeking is causing you to search,"** so you may as well just get on with it.

PREPARATION

- Block out three 30 minute sessions in your diary over the next seven days.

- Start a training journal to record your meditation practice sessions and to make any notes or observations.

- Choose the time you are going to sit quietly without distractions or interference.

- Find a room with a bare or plain floor or wall, without patterns, pictures or sticky notes.

- You'll need a hard-backed, armless chair with a padded seat or cushion to sit on, so find one that is suitable for the purpose.

- If you need to let other people know what you're doing and get their help and support, or for them to vacate the area, sort this out ahead of time.

- When the time arrives, put your phone and other devices on silent or sleep mode; but you'll need a timer, so you could use this function on your mobile phone or watch, for example.

PRACTICE GUIDELINES

- Get comfortable.

- You may want to open the window, loosen your shirt collar and belt and kick off your shoes.

- Place your chair approximately three feet away from a blank wall or the back of a door, or use a room with a plain floor, as you'll be sitting with your eyes open and will want to minimise distractions.

- Set your timer for 15 to 20 minutes and then put it to the side or behind you so that you can't see it.

- Relax and prepare yourself to be quiet for the next quarter of an hour, as a minimum.

- Give yourself permission to do nothing but sit quietly with yourself.

- Don't force anything, don't change anything, simply observe yourself and how busy your mind most likely is.

- Observe the tensions in your body.

- Stay with the impressions of tension and a busy mind without trying to change anything.

- Allow your breath to simply come and go without interference.

- Gradually awaken to a stronger physical sensation of yourself sitting in your chair.

- As you become more settled in your body, continue to follow your breathing, noticing how it becomes deeper and slows down.

- You might feel sleepy but remember your task is to train your attention, watch your breathing and discipline your mind to follow this fundamental action.

- Every time you get distracted and disappear into your thoughts, make the effort to come back to your breathing and into the present moment.

- Sit like this until your timer goes off, signalling the end of the practice session.

NB. This style of meditation advocates that you practise with your eyes open and your feet on the floor, rather than the more traditional way of sitting cross-legged on a cushion with your eyes closed. There are many reasons for this, not least of which is that you'll want to apply it to your golf (although the benefits will reach far beyond your game). So you'll want to be aware of your feet on the ground at address and be able to look towards the target, all the while maintaining the state of relaxed attention you're cultivating with your daily practice.

JUST SITTING

Commonly known as 'Zen', this is the Japanese pronunciation of the earlier Chinese term 'Chan' – derived originally from the Sanskrit 'dhyana', which may be translated as sitting meditation or mental concentration upon a single object, most notably the breath and its action.

The Chinese word '*Chan*' describes a form of Mahayana Buddhist teaching founded by Bodhidharma, an Indian monk who arrived in China in the late fifth century.

It describes the process of seeing into the stillness of one's Original Nature, which is undisturbed by thinking.

By the seventh century, Chan was the dominant method of meditation and was later transmitted from China, first to Korea and then to Japan, where it is known as Sen and Zen respectively.

Zen is better known in the west, due to the spread of Japanese Buddhism after the second world war when religious freedom on mainland China was severely restricted.

In each case, the utmost importance is placed on single-mindedly following the breath in accordance with the Buddha's teachings, thus allowing the practitioner to encounter the oneness of their Original Nature.

HOW TO PRACTISE

1. Sit upright and towards the front edge of your chair. Your feet are positioned on the ground in front of the knees, opening the angle to minimise strain on the knee joints.

2. Your palms are resting on your thighs or cupped in your lap (left-hand palm up inside the right palm for women; right-hand palm up inside the left palm for men) and your thumbs are touching.

3. Tuck your chin in and hold the crown of your head up, as if it were held by a thread. Relax your face, empty your chest and loosen your shoulders.

4. Keep your eyes open and simply look ahead and slightly downwards, at the floor or the wall at a distance of approximately 3ft to 5ft, depending on what's comfortable. You are not trying to stare, but let your gaze rest gently.

5. Lower your awareness to your navel area (t'an tien) and feel the sensation of breathing in and breathing out. Do not force your breathing; just relax and allow your diaphragm to expand so your breathing becomes deep and horizontal.

6. As you sit, thoughts will come into your mind and you will soon forget to focus on your breathing. This may take just a few moments. Gently bring your awareness back to your breathing and continue.

7. Feel the sensation of air filling and emptying from the body or listen to the sound of your breath entering and exiting the nostrils.

8. As you sit you may develop a stronger impression of your physical body, particularly your feet, legs and back. These sensations can encourage you to stay in the present moment and strengthen your attention.

9. Continue sitting like this, bringing your awareness back to your breathing, each time you get distracted and your mind starts to wander.

Just Sitting

Drawing: Kristin Rawcliffe

ENDING THE SESSION

When your timer goes off, have a little stretch and stand up slowly and carefully. Walk about the room for a few minutes or, if you can, go outside in nature. Try not to throw away all your hard work but retain something of your practice as you start to move quietly back into the everyday pace of life. You may like to get a cup of tea and make a few notes in your training journal, but be careful not to judge or analyse the quality of your practice; simply continue day by day.

DAILY PRACTICE

Given the frenetic pace of modern life and the fact that we are now so used to demanding instant results and satisfaction at the push of a button or the swipe of a screen, how can we approach this work that demands consistent, daily effort?

I regularly receive messages from golfers who have had spectacular results on the course from their initial attempts at this training (shooting five pars or birdies in a row, an all-time low of 78, the best round of golf ever, winning for the first time, etc). But many then get frustrated at the thought of continuing with the practice because they still want to (1) get it right; (2) force it to happen; (3) analyse it; and (4) look for results.

All the same problems that interfere with the delivery of a fluid golf shot and brought them to this training in the first place.

Yet it seems that people just can't help bringing these same attitudes into their practice of meditation; perhaps because that's the default setting of the western mind – and one which we are trying to dissipate through our following of the breath.

What's coming into play also is the mind's refusal to give up its mistaken belief that it already knows, and therefore that meditation can be approached in just the same way as any other area in our lives where we are trying to be successful, and where we can use our willpower to make something happen.

This is a humbling path and one that asks you simply to do the practice – sitting quietly, following your breathing for 15 to 20 minutes a day.

It's simple, but not easy. This journey is for the most part a journey into the unknown. It's a journey that will take you beyond the ordinary, everyday mind and into the realm of the mind-body connection. From here you will have the ability to deliver golf shots that are fluid, powerful, effortless and precise, so that you can perform, even under pressure and win.

But it all starts with sitting quietly each and every day.

To begin with, I'd advise you to practise three times a week, most especially on days when you are heading either to the range or to the course. As you get accustomed to this new rhythm in your life, you can increase the number of your sessions so that you are practising daily.

However, you don't want to become so attached to the training that you bring the wrong approach into your practice. I learned this the hard way many years ago by promising myself that I would sit every day for 100 days, no matter what, but on the half a dozen or so days when it was impossible due to my schedule, family matters, feeling unwell and so forth, I got really uptight and annoyed that I couldn't sit.

On other days when life was difficult and there wasn't much time to sit, I knew I was forcing the practice just to fit it into the day. Both scenarios of course are the antithesis of what meditation is all about. Subsequently I learned that even monks don't sit on calendar dates with the numbers four or nine in them, which are traditionally days of relaxed schedule in Zen monasteries. So it's useful to have downtime to refresh, regroup and reaffirm your commitment.

Above all, you need sincerity to find your way and to be honest with yourself about when it's not possible to sit as opposed to when you simply don't feel like sitting. The value of sitting when you don't feel like it cannot be overstated.

So you need to be vigilant with yourself and with your practice. It's important to understand why you're doing it and it's also important to see how difficult it is to do this simplest of things – sitting quietly for 15 to 20 minutes, following your breathing. Seeing the struggle is part of the practice, as without witnessing the constant stream of unwanted thoughts there will be no attempt to detach from them.

Training your mind to be quiet and developing your attention to focus on a single task are disciplines that require commitment, similar to that necessary for toning your muscles or losing body fat in the gym. The effort to train or practise daily has its own rewards, and will help to create a thread of constancy, of neutrality, and a more resolute inner strength that will run through your life and your golf game, no matter the highs and lows.

With daily practice you will learn to reduce mental interference, to bring your mind more under your control while seeing the fickleness of your thoughts, moods and emotions, all the while building something up inside that these fluctuating mood states can't destroy.

Remember it's not a mental game technique, it's a practice. With meditation you will practise every day to enter the doorway to the zone; but you can't then think your way into this doorway when you're playing golf. You simply have to keep doing the practice, keep focusing on the breath, coming back to it again and again while you're going through your pre-shot routine, stepping up to the ball, walking away from a poor shot, talking with your playing partners, writing on your score card, accepting the trophy and giving your victory speech.

But don't make the mistake of doing this training only to get results on the golf course; you cannot meditate while at the same time looking for results. Undoubtedly results will come, but something has to precede that: your own transformation, an inner quiet, more self-understanding, and mastery of your ever-changing internal landscape. All these things will enable you to play a better game, but your focus needs to be on your practice.

Buddhist monks try never to leave their place of meditation, so that even after their morning sitting is over, they still maintain an inner attitude of quiet vigilance.

Similarly, over time you'll find the inner peace attained during your practice will stay longer and longer after your practice has finished, but first you'll need to build a training routine.

BUILDING A ROUTINE

I've practised formal Buddhist meditation for decades and through the many joys and sorrows that life can bring. When I started, I had no idea that I would still be doing it today. There was a time when I felt continually sleepy during my practice, yet I persisted. I practised while living in a house with a 'special needs' adult where there was little or no peace and quiet. I've trained in a house-share where I was laughed at for "going to stare at the wall", when losing my beloved Mum suddenly to a stroke, through my subsequent relationship break-up, being forced to move home, through illness, injury and financial hardships and through rebuilding my life and business. I did my practice this morning before sitting down to write.

It's amazing to think that I have got what it takes to have done this, but then perhaps it was the daily practice that gave me the inner strength in the first place. We know that the brain changes with regular meditation practice. Magnetic resonance imaging (MRI) studies have shown thickening of parts of the brain's outer layer, the cortex, after several weeks of meditation. This could explain why meditators find that, after some time, it becomes easier to meditate as you develop 'meditation muscles'.

My routine has always been to sit either first thing in the morning or at the end of the working day (or both) and this has usually been planned ahead of time to fit in with my training and fitness regime, teaching and family commitments and time spent writing.

Building the days up one by one creates a cumulative effect, which creates a reservoir of calm that goes deeper than the mind can perceive or understand. Where you are now and where you'll end up with your practice are likely poles apart; while nothing will seemingly change, everything changes as you become more and more tolerant and forgiving of yourself and others and have more acceptance of everything life can throw at you.

We take only ourselves into our sport. You don't become someone different when you walk out to the first tee; in fact, golf can act like a mirror and magnify all your faults and foibles as the dominant traits of your personality come to the fore, especially when you're in contention.

Hesitant people have difficulty committing to the shot; over-thinkers can't let go of swing thoughts; those who can't control their emotions break clubs in frustration. You get the picture. With meditation practice, you can simply observe these tendencies in yourself but learn to stay calm, neutral and dispassionate without giving into them.

The zone or flow-state is already there, hardwired into your brain and nervous system; it just needs activating by your willingness to breathe deeply and slowly and to train your attention rather than letting it run riot so you go through a maelstrom of emotions and ricochet back and forth with your thoughts on each and every shot.

Any time of the day is a good time to practise so you need to find your own way, maybe getting up half an hour earlier or doing it as soon as you get in from work.

If you can prearrange this with yourself and make a pact with your partner, housemate or work colleagues, telling them what you're doing and hopefully getting their support, you'll have more chance of sticking with it, especially when you're just starting out on your journey.

Remember the days and the years are going to tick by anyhow, whether you do the practice or not, but how much more joy will you experience in your golf game and your everyday life if you use the days and the years to hone your attention and bring peace to your mind.

You already have an idea of what are you going to face: irritation, boredom, sleepiness, an inability to focus, frustration, believing there are more important things that you need to do with your time, and so on.

Just know what to expect; observe yourself without buying into these negative thoughts and destructive emotions and simply follow your breathing.

The willingness to fall down again and again and just keep going is the stuff champions are made of and of course the Buddhists have a saying for this attitude when applied to the practice of meditation, **"Under all circumstances, continue."**

TRY THIS:

- Write your meditation sessions in your diary as you do with any other appointment and make the commitment to honour these self-promises.

- Practise first thing in the morning before going to work or otherwise starting your day.

- Sit quietly when your working day is done and before your evening recreational activities.

- Schedule time to practise ahead of every round of golf; this could be done at home or in the office or even in the car. You might like to practise when you come off the course as a way of dispelling any negative thoughts about how you played.

NB. It's not a good idea to sit before you go to bed, even though at first your practice may leave you feeling sleepy as it can have a soporific effect. The idea behind this training is to wake up to yourself in the present moment and to be fully alert yet calm when you play golf. As you continue with your training, you'll enter the coveted state of 'relaxed concentration' typical of the zone or flow state, which is not to be used as a precursor for sleep.

INTRODUCING DISTRACTIONS

For your first 66 days (the amount of time research shows is needed to form a new habit) you will be doing your daily practice undisturbed. You've got the buy-in from family, friends and co-workers and have a quiet place to go to at your designated time to sit quietly and follow your breathing. You'll have logged the days in your training journal, building up a routine.

Now is the time to start introducing distractions.

This natural progression in your training is to help you maintain a Zen-like state when you're out on the course in contention and you have the gallery, clubhouse spectators, opponents or playing partners as well as the weather to contend with.

Ultimately you are going to learn how to divide your attention (we'll get to this in the next chapter), so that you can retain part of your awareness on your breathing all the time you're playing golf. But unless you train your attention by knuckling down and doing your daily practice, this will be a great idea instead of an experience akin to the zone on the golf course.

So what sort of distractions am I talking about?

Not looking for the perfect place or conditions in which to do your meditation – for example, sitting on the edge of the bath, the kitchen stool or in your car; being hungry or otherwise physically uncomfortable, or doing your practice while others carry on with their activities around you.

We know that the brainwaves of someone in deep meditation and a golfer or other athlete performing 'in the zone' are in the alpha state; here there is little or no mental interference by way of the internal dialogue and similarly there is little self-talk about external irritations. You can hear your children playing or the television programme in the next room, but you don't have to become irked and annoyed by it.

The ability to see how often and how continually you are pulled away from the present moment and the breath you are taking is invaluable. You are breathing all the time throughout all your activities; all you need to do is remember that you are breathing and remember over and over and over again.

The value of this on the course is that you'll be able to build up a quiet place inside where you can go to when your playing partners are chatting while you're trying to prepare for your shot, or when somebody offers unsolicited advice on your grip, or you start to feel anxious because your second shot was a bit wayward and has ended up in the bunker.

If you can stay with your breathing, everything else will settle down: thoughts are not so dominant, emotions are not so heightened, problems don't seem to have the same hold on you, you are happier, you seem to have more space inside, your head isn't so crowded and it feels as though you have more time. You will also have far more ability to swing a golf club with fluidity, power and grace.

Training this ability by introducing distractions while continually coming back to the breath establishes a quiet place inside that anchors you in the present moment.

Remember the image of a candle flame, constantly flickering on the verge of going out. With your attention focused on your breathing you can keep the flame steady, holding it as a centre point around which everything else revolves.

"Keep your mind within yourself" is a Tai Chi adage I heard many years ago and one that's always stuck with me. It may help you to recognise how often the mind is scattered as we are continually pulled away from being where we actually are.

Aim to practise remembering your breathing throughout the day, for instance when you're driving, when you're talking on the phone, when you're watching a film and when you're standing waiting on the tee.

How often have you remembered to follow your breath while you're reading this book?

See what has the most power to take you away from your breathing. Is it your thoughts, are you beset by negativity and worry, are you a fidgeter, a nail-biter or a daydreamer, or are you somebody who automatically goes into their emotions at the slightest provocation?

Notice what takes you away from your breathing in your everyday life and you'll undoubtedly see these are exactly the traits that take you away from being relaxed, ready and *present* over the ball when you're playing golf.

This process of self-observation goes hand-in-hand with meditation training; to observe your breathing, to see how often you get pulled away from being in the now and to recognise what it is that's taking you, will help you to hone the stillness that's prerequisite before any pure strike of the ball.

Remember, the breath is what unites the mind and body; so witness the quality of your breathing when you're anxious at set-up and you're feeling uptight or rushed, as opposed to how you're breathing when you hit the perfect shot.

The circle of excellence (p60) clearly shows a correlation between the ability to breathe deeply and slowly and the internal conditions necessary for fluid motion to occur. The more you can pay attention to how this manifests itself in your performance when you're on the course, the more on track you'll be to winning games.

TRY THIS:

- Try practising at different times of the day so that your daily meditation doesn't become just another habit.

- Extend the length of your practice sessions from 20 to 30 minutes.

- Sit when you are tired or hungry or when you're uncomfortable; this is invaluable training to keep the mind steady and the emotions neutral and emulates the formal practice of Buddhist monasteries, particularly in Japan.

- Practise when there are other people around or when there is background noise or disturbance.

- Sit quietly in the locker room ahead of the game, no matter what other players might think.

NB. Many athletes make their training sessions harder than the actual feat they're competing in: for instance, sprint distance runners train by running on sand, which is noticeably harder and more wearing on the legs than running on a race track. Similarly, *by making your meditation sessions ever more challenging, you'll be training yourself to stay detached and keep your attention in the present moment by following your breathing, no matter what's going on inside or around you.*

PART FOUR

DEEP PRACTICE

"To master our breath is to be in control of our bodies and minds. Each time we find ourselves dispersed and find it difficult to gain control of ourselves by different means, the method of watching the breath should always be used."

Thich Nhat Hanh

DIVIDING YOUR ATTENTION

The importance of daily meditation is nowhere more apparent than when applying breathing awareness to your golf practice time. If you can't do it here, you won't be able to do it when you're out on the course, and the ability will be all but lost during those pressure shots, along with your chance of victory.

Every moment of every day you are breathing, yet your attention is taken by the distractions of the outside world and the noise of your own inner landscape, which includes your thoughts, dreams, memories and emotions.

Meditation is the easiest thing in the world to talk about and so-called 'meditation apps' have thousands of followers, but what will separate you from the herd and help you to experience real-life tangible effects in your game is to actually do the training in a more formal and considered way. This will distinguish not only the men from the boys, so to speak, but also the winners from the losers.

We do not remember the breath, we do not remember ourselves, and we do not include awareness of the breath in our activities. Sometimes we even hold the breath, so unconscious of it are we; and considering that the breath is the only thing keeping us alive, this is a very sorry state of affairs.

Finding time each day to practise paying attention to your breathing is the only way to become conscious of this automatic process – and it's only by making it conscious that you can then harness it for your game. All the while the breath remains unconscious, your performance level will stay where it is and the chances are that your game may even deteriorate as the only recourses available to you will be your mind (which cannot control movement) and your technique (which won't flow if your mind and body are disconnected).

Dividing your attention is the process of staying conscious of your breathing while simultaneously focusing on your current activity; in other words, it's a dividing of your attention between your interior and the outside world. Like meditation itself, this is so much easier said than done, but it is possible when we make enough effort.

In your game, this means striving to be aware of your breathing, watching it and allowing each breath to be deep, slow and quiet while you're doing anything and everything from walking to the first tee, taking your practice swings, stepping up to the ball and so forth.

It also means not losing yourself in your activity, nor disappearing into your mind with its imagined promise of angles, swing plane and the physics of the perfect shot.

It means staying *present* and alert to yourself, without getting swallowed up by your emotions – this is crucial, because as Fred Shoemaker (*Extraordinary Golf*) has pointed out, most golfers are constantly on the verge of being upset.

Where you breathe from is vital too; shallow breathing as we've seen serves only to initiate the stress response, causing feelings of anxiety and promoting tension in the body. Long, slow, deep breaths encourage the opposite of this, engage the relaxation response and with it the alpha state or Zen-mind, which is the essential requirement for effortless shot-making.

Retaining part of your attention on your breathing, and staying with the sensation of your body, particularly the t'an tien, serves to activate the zone, allowing fluid motion to flow seamlessly from your mind (your intention for the shot), through your body (the motion of swing) and into the clubhead to strike the ball.

It's a gradual process and one that needs training as the attention can be held in this way only for a matter of moments; remember that 12 seconds is the estimated time any one of us can be 'in the now', so you need to keep working to enable another 12 seconds and another and another all the time you're on the golf course.

The French writer and philosopher Jean-Paul Sartre once said, "Hell is other people", but the feedback I've had from hundreds of players suggests that hell is playing golf with the various parts of yourself (mind, body, emotions) disconnected, scattered and warring with each other, while clutching on to ideas you have about swing plane.

It's frustrating, debilitating and demoralising to play the game this way because you instinctively know you can do better and most likely have played better in the past; if only you could remember what you were doing when you 'accidentally' experienced the zone or flow and with it the effortless shot.

Remembering how is as simple as remembering your breath, remembering that when you focus on your breathing your mind quietens down, your emotions are neutralised and your body relaxes.

This is what you must focus on when you're playing, over and above thoughts of spine angle and club trajectories; dividing your attention so that you're aware of yourself breathing, noticing perhaps that the breath is short and shallow as you stand over a clutch putt and summoning your effort spent in daily practice to bring the breath into the lower body, relax your grip and hole out for the trophy.

TRY THIS:

- Practise meditation for the usual length of time, but while looking at a golf ball on the floor a few feet in front of you. Divide your attention between following your breathing and noticing the ball's shape, contours, any shadows that it casts, the dimples on its surface, the logo etc. Don't talk to yourself about the ball, just look at it with quiet dispassion while you continue to follow your breathing.

- Whatever activity you perform after your meditation practice, from preparing tea, to washing up, sending emails or making a phone call, try to stay with the divided awareness of paying attention to whatever you're doing while at the same time following your breathing.

- Schedule a daily appointment with yourself, at the same time each day when you will try to be present in your breath plus whatever else you're doing. Don't be surprised if you forget more often than you remember, but try to learn something about why meditation practice is so important if you are to use your breathing successfully to raise your golf performance.

SELF-OBSERVATION

Or: "Why is it that my practice swing can feel fluid and effortless, but when I step up to the ball and have to make the shot, everything changes... for the worse?"

Have you ever had this experience on the golf course?

You're about to play a shot with your favourite iron and you do a couple of easy, slow-tempo practice swings with a beautiful rhythm and a lovely, balanced finish, but when you actually come to hit the ball, your swing somehow changes and all the faults you've tried so hard to correct come back with a vengeance as you either slice or top the ball or otherwise play a duff shot?

Of course you have. It's one of the enduring enigmas about the game, which has baffled even the most legendary players, like Bobby Jones, who said, "Golf is assuredly a mystifying game. It would seem that if a person has hit a golf ball correctly a thousand times, he should be able to duplicate the performance at will. But such is certainly not the case."

And what are these faults that show up time and again? Working with my students, I've noticed these include (but are certainly not limited to) rushing, shortening the backswing, lack of extension, overuse of the upper body, flicking the wrists, poor balance and no follow-through. However, these faults are simply the external manifestations of the internal mind-body disconnection, which itself is the result of shallow breathing, which in turn activates the stress response and contributes to the circle of deterioration (p59).

The mainstream approach to fixing this problem is of course to have more golf lessons, change your swing coach, and read tips and tricks online or in the golf media in an attempt to learn more about the mechanics, angles and geometry of the swing. Obviously, the thinking goes, you've duffed the shot as you've overlooked an important technical point, which if you could just rectify once and for all, you'll finally have your game sorted right? Wrong!

Many golfers I've worked with, from competitive amateurs to seasoned professionals and coaches who've been involved with the game over a lifetime, have all realised that golf, truly effortless golf, is first and foremost a game of breathing, the quality of which determines the quality of the mind-body connection and with it the quality of the swing.

What these players have noticed, using the type of insight that can only come through the practice of self-observation, is the correlation between breathing and the rhythm, timing and execution of the shot.

Without working to master the breath, golfers remain prey to a whole gamut of physiological and psychological changes, which occur from moment to moment and from shot to shot, which disrupt the fluidity of movement and cause changes in the motion of the club, no matter how much the player knows about technique.

Ultimately, syncing the mind and body via the medium of the breath is the only way to flow.

TRY THIS:

- Notice your breathing while you make your practice swings and how the movement of the club feels as a result. Now notice any changes that occur when you swing for real. For instance, does the breath become shorter or stuck in the upper chest? Maybe you stop breathing altogether?

- How does your grip compare with your breathing? Do they both get tighter and how does this affect your ability to move freely through the swing? Are you breathing quickly and does this internal tempo then force you to rush the shot?

SHOT PREPARATION

A huge stumbling block for many golfers when they first begin this 'alternative' eastern-style of training is that they make the mistake of not trusting it entirely, but trying to have a foot in both worlds as they cling on to the mainstream approach while half-heartedly 'doing the breathing' piecemeal or as and when they remember.

However, this 'deep practice' approach is above all one of constancy as your golf practice, shot preparation and on-course performance all have the same fundamental requirement: the slow, deliberate and attentive use of breathing awareness, which itself demands regular daily practice.

Focusing on the breath to quieten the mind and encourage fluid motion works all the time in all situations and scenarios so long as you do the training, but then you have to give yourself to it. As Zen master Shunryu Suzuki says, "When you do something, you should burn yourself up completely, like a good bonfire, leaving no trace of yourself."

You can't think about your breath in the same way that you think about technique, because the true impulse to follow the breathing exerts a very different demand on the attention as it cancels out analytical thinking altogether. You may kid yourself that you're using your breathing as you stand over the ball clutching your driver, but thinking about breathing is anathema to flow.

Here it might be useful to understand a concept that Jack Kornfield (Vipassana meditation teacher and author of *A Path With Heart*) calls the spiritual 'near enemy', whereby one quality masquerades as its opposite. For instance, he cites attachment as the near enemy of loving kindness; pity the near enemy of compassion; comparison the near enemy of sympathy; indifference the near enemy of equanimity.

In terms of breathing or just thinking about breathing, one of my students explained it thus:

"I need to reorient my mind away from expectations about results and towards the practice and the enjoyment of effortlessness. I am still learning the difference between just doing it and doing it by following instructions, doing what Jayne says, directing myself, listening to a voice. I am getting better at coming back to myself, but there is a difference between coming back to a self that is breathing and aware, and coming back to a self who is the 'director', who says 'focus on your t'an tien' and who transforms into an abusive critic the moment the shot does not come off properly. I feel this 'director' self is a near enemy of the breathing and aware self. He hangs out in the same place, behind the monkey mind, and arises when I call on the breathing self. So I will keep practising and see what I can do with him."

Martin D - Ireland

TRY THIS:

- Practise staying aware of your breathing as you pull your club from the bag. Try this 10 times as a drill until you can breathe in while lifting the club and breathe out as you lightly form your grip around the shaft. Remember to stay focused on the t'an tien/navel area to stop the breath rising into the upper chest.

- As you decide which shot you're going to play, try to stay with your body so that you don't get completely lost in your analytical mind. Feel your grip with just the right amount of pressure or the sensation of your feet on the ground together with the rhythm of slow, deep breaths.

- At set-up, simply ask yourself the Karl Morris 'Quality Question', "What does a good shot look like here?" You will most likely find that an image of a shot appears in your mind's eye. It may be the shape of the ideal shot that you picture, you may answer it verbally or you may get a sense or a feeling of the shot you'd like to make. Working this approach together with your breathing will give you the best chance of taking the wonderful and unique opportunity your mind gives you to 'preprogramme' the shot you want to make, mentally rehearsing it and then executing it with the finesse that only the mind-body connection can summon.

> • Start your Nicklaus-style visualisation sequence (p70) only once you've tuned into your breathing and cleared your mind. Try to think in pictures rather than words and stay with the cadence of your breathing while envisioning the shot.

BREATHING YOUR SWING

As we've seen, the golf swing is one of the most complex sequences of movement in all of sport, a multifaceted sequential event demanding specific yet progressive neurological and muscular firing resulting in the release of coiled explosive power to impact a 1.62-inch ball (British size).

It's been written about, analysed and scrutinised more than any other motion in sport and it's in this that most of the game's problems lie. As a seasoned coach and player once told me, every new young pro coming up thinks they are going to find the secret to better even the likes of Hogan and Nicklaus by finding the one key, one angle, one turn of the screw in the golfing machine that's been overlooked by others... but of course this is never going to happen.

The reason Hogan and Nicklaus were outstanding as champions is that they worked it out with their bodies, not with preconceived ideas in their minds: Nicklaus with his deliberate attention to posture at address, a slow take-away and emphasis on swing feelings; and Hogan with his slow-motion practice, obsessing over what worked and what didn't as he used his body to dig the ball out of the dirt.

Watching today's elite as well as recreational golfers at any club you care to mention, the one overriding thing I always notice (in the men's game especially) is the amount of tension players carry in the face, chest, arms and shoulders. This of course negates any ability they might have to breathe deeply and move with fluidity – a situation that's often compounded (again in the men's game) by excessive upper-body weightlifting in a misguided attempt to gain extra power.

Where is this tension coming from? Mostly from trying to get right the technical points that have been learned in lessons and during practice sessions, and then using this same analytical mindset when taking the game to the course.

Could it also be that the ego needs to protect itself against what other people think and that the stress response is compounded by the fear of getting it wrong, the anxiety about looking stupid and so forth, which then contributes to the default setting of trying too hard and thinking too much? Well, yes!

Somehow the ability to focus on the breathing means a shift away from the ego, from a self that dominates with thoughts of achievement and looking good.

Any time you have an overriding thought or an intent that is entirely mental, it activates the prefrontal cortex and interrupts the signal to the motor system, throwing off the complex chain of motion that has to occur seamlessly and without any mental interference for your swing, chip shot or putting stoke to be fluid and precise.

You simply cannot force the perfect shot or make it happen with an effort of your willpower; all you can do is work to create the right internal conditions that will enable this experience to occur.

Allowing your swing to be dictated by your breathing, rather than your mind and your ego, is to come under a different influence, one which allows your nervous system to switch from stress to relaxation and alters the very state of the relationship between your mind and body.

But it can occur only when you get out of your own way and relinquish control and that can often be a scary place to be. This is perhaps why many prefer to talk about breathing and use gadgets and gizmos that light up when the brainwaves accidentally switch to the alpha state, rather than make a daily commitment to the practice of meditation.

TRY THIS:

- **Awareness of breathing during your pre-shot routine**

  The mind works on many levels simultaneously, so while sizing up the shot, picking your target, choosing your club and adjusting your grip, maintain awareness on your t'an tien (navel area) while breathing slowly, deeply and horizontally. This will ensure that your nervous system stays in the relaxation mode and will stop you feeling anxious, especially when putting.

- **Internal awareness when addressing the ball**

  1. **Empty your chest**: emptying or hollowing the chest is the first key to developing balance as it relaxes the upper body, freeing the neck, releasing the shoulders and emptying the lungs. You'll find that exhaling deeply is a natural part of this process, which releases pent up anxiety and tension.

  2. **Focus on the t'an tien**: lowering your centre of awareness, by concentrating your mind on the navel, is extremely useful for your golf. As you gently focus on your navel, you will find that you start to breathe more deeply and this in turn sends increased oxygen along with your 'feel-good' chemical signals (endorphins) to your brain. It also gets you in touch with your centre of gravity, and enhances lower-body stability.

3. **Sink into the feet**: eastern philosophy (and quantum physics) tells us that energy (Chi) follows attention (Yi); thus, when you focus on your lower body you will feel more stable and rooted. A key principle from Tai Chi is to relax the upper body and allow the legs to support the torso, which is great for balance and adding power and distance to your drives.

• **Awareness of breathing during your swing**

Focus on breathing in while you take the club away slowly, then breathe out as you hit down and through the ball, with strong and deliberate intent, making sure to keep your awareness on your navel area throughout the motion. This will help you to keep your mind within yourself and engage your lower body so that it leads the transition from the top.

Martial artists always breathe out when they strike (punch or kick), thus delivering 20 to 30% more energy through the target.

Here's some recent feedback from a new student, a seasoned golfer who's just started training in breath-centred meditation and is enjoying the feeling of freedom this is giving him in his swing:

"It feels better when I put most of my focus on my breathing while playing. My body has a tendency to flip the wrists and forearms rather than rotate them. This has been a long-term habit or pattern. When I feel the arms rotate versus flip, my ball striking improves. A few times during the round I felt my body become totally relaxed and fluid from my breathing. It was very distinct but fleeting… when my breathing is slow and consistent my motion follows suit. When my breathing becomes rapid, so does my swing and I tend to hook my shots." **Howie K. - California**

Chi: energy, life force or breath

SHORT GAME SAMURAI

In the eastern martial and meditative arts the focus is always on the process and the posture, so that we habituate or associate the correct posture with breathing deeply, and gathering our attention, so we can be centred. This applies when we are in stillness, when preparing for movement and when in motion.

For instance, in sitting meditation the posture and the practice are aligned so that when we sit and hold our body in a particular way – head up, spine straight, shoulders relaxed, mind at the navel – this triggers a memory of previous practice and helps to focus the attention.

Even in the Korean art of horseback archery, the focus of the warrior rider is still on their meditation posture and their breathing, even when they are thundering along on the back of a stallion. Sure, they aim at the target as they race past it, but the focus is always on the posture and breathing.

How great would it be to experience this in your golf game, with a pre-shot and set-up routine that encouraged unification between your mind and body, that was both enlivening and relaxing and gave you access to the flow state before you even took your shot? If you've been keeping up and have started your daily practice, you'll know that's what this whole book is all about.

So in meditation, the posture *is* the practice, and we focus on the process not the results, keeping awareness of breathing as paramount. In your golf game this attitude encourages a seamless transition from stillness (set-up) into movement (the shot) using the breath as the one true constant.

The short game can make or break a player: it's the game within a game where the emphasis changes from power (off the tee), distance and ball placement (your iron shots), to controlled creativity, touch and feel (chipping and putting).

The closer the ball gets to the hole, the more nerves, anxiety and mental interference can come to the fore, but these things, as you're finding out, are activated and can also therefore be subdued by a change in your breathing.

Shallow, quick and short breaths into your upper chest – the result of perceived stress and its threat to the ego (worrying about missing the putt and what other people think) – is hardwired into our nervous systems as the stress response, along with its opposite, the relaxation response.

This is another crucial area where the practice of self-observation can help you. Catching yourself and noticing how your breath changes as you approach your chip shot or walk on to the green is the first step to short game mastery.

You need to get conscious and really see what's happening, using not the realm of your thoughts as the starting place but the realm of your mind-body connection.

The way you breathe and how conscious (or otherwise) you are of your breathing changes everything: it changes how your nervous-system responds; it alters your pulse and heart rate; it affects whether your muscles are pliable or tight; it determines how much sensation or awareness you have of yourself; whether you can feel the green underneath your feet; and it affects your grip pressure. It basically changes everything to do with how you prepare for and execute movement.

Once activated, the relaxation response will negate all the anxiety, even the fear, associated with the short clutch putt. It will help you to develop trust, to stop second-guessing yourself or looking at the hole too much and will help you commit to the shot with a quiet confidence.

It is also the antidote to the yips.

The t'an tien (navel) plays a crucial role on the greens too. This area, which I like to think of as the 'chi core', is the centre-point of movement in the three Chinese *internal* martial arts of Tai Chi, Hsing and Bagua. In these arts, the body's centre of gravity directs movement, which always starts as a clear idea or intention formed in the mind.

To understand how the chi core can work in your short game, imagine a triangle formed by joining a straight line connecting your feet with two more straight lines (one from each foot) meeting at the navel. According to the most ancient wisdom from the martial arts, this lower-body triangle is where all movement should begin with the upper body simply following the turning of the navel and the shifting distribution of weight in the feet.

Therefore, the mainstream approach to putting, which emphasises the movement of the shoulders (which form an upper-body triangle with the chi core), is actually counter to biomechanical principles. The pros get away with it because of the amount of time they spend playing golf, but for the average player this approach can only be a source of frustration.

Let me give you an example.

I was working with my student Erik on the putting green and asked him to putt the five balls we were using for practice. He took his time and set up in his usual way, but missed every one, some by only a small margin, but nevertheless none of the balls found their way to the bottom of the cup.

After a short time explaining the lower-body triangle, encouraging Erik to breathe deeply, empty his chest, engage with his core and feel his feet on the ground, I asked him to try again and to close his eyes this time before taking each shot, to really develop instinct, trust and feel.

This time he holed four of the five putts.

There is a very strong correlation between deep breathing and a body that is stable, balanced and able to move freely, and the short game is where your commitment to the daily practice of meditation will really pay off. The more you do your training, the more inner reserves you will have to call upon when you're standing on the green about to take a crucial putt that could seal your fate as the next club champion.

Psychological and mental game techniques are just that: they are of the mind and work only on the mind. All the various procedures, no matter how brilliantly they may work in the short term, will need changing or reworking at some point so the monkey mind can be re-engaged and have something new to keep it occupied.

With breath-centred meditation it is different: the more you practise, the more real changes are effected in the nervous system, your brain is rewired, your stress threshold increases, anxiety falls away and there is an uptake of happiness and acceptance. The brain has a certain plasticity that allows the regular meditator to instigate real and lasting changes, but only – you guessed it – if you consistently train your brain with regular daily practice. Otherwise you'll be in the same old default state, which is a sorry combination of autopilot, over-thinking and scattered attention; not at all the mindset you want to take on to the greens.

As you continue to practise, you will experience first-hand how something is built up: an inner calm, resilience, the ability to ignore negative thoughts and mental chatter, to get centred, to pause, to prepare, to observe, to have a clear head, and to manage yourself and the course alike.

It's always been my contention that you don't need a magic headband to get your brainwaves in the alpha state, although I understand that some people may like to use these devices as a visual aid to show the internal state they're working towards.

However, there is no substitute for traditional, formal meditation practice, which also builds character, self-reliance and an ability to cope with pressures – all the qualities you need when you're standing alone on the 18th green with a chance to hole out for the championship.

You cannot force the short game; you cannot make the putt happen by using willpower and might or any other ego-led attempt to get the ball in the hole. The shot will be successful only when you get out of your own way, and that means anchoring your attention on your breathing, allowing mind and body, thinking and technique finally to come together.

TRY THIS:

- Taking your lead from the great Samurai swordsman Miyamoto Musashi, who trained a 'ready stance' rather than fighting techniques, focus on the posture required to activate true biomechanical principles that will withstand pressure. Again, these principles are to relax your upper body, specifically your chest and shoulders, engage your chi core with lower-abdominal breathing and feel your feet on the ground.

- Practise visualising a lower-body triangle, which is formed from your navel, down into each foot, which are also connected. Focusing in this way will increase your lower-body stability and start the process of using the t'an tien as a fulcrum for the motion of your shot.

- Research shows that the most successful short game players access the alpha state (p66), the brainwave pattern of 9 to 12 cycles per second, which activates the zone or flow, negating anxiety and allowing the body to move freely. Aim to quieten your mind before you take your shot by breathing deeply to shut down the prefrontal cortex, the role of which as analytical thinker will hinder your ability to flow.

- You may have seen kung fu films where the method of 'sticky hands' is practised by exponents who are blindfolded. The idea behind this is to help the practitioner develop instinct and intuition, which is far more powerful than the logical mind. Practise putting with your eyes closed to develop feeling, sensitivity and trust, which helps to override the analytical mind's desire to hesitate and second-guess.

My student Jeremy practised eyes-closed putting alongside his daily meditation and wrote to me after he had won his first major competition:

"So it happened… I played in a competition on Saturday and won it! This is the first major competition I have ever won! I shot one over par and won by two shots. I used the standing meditation technique on the last five holes when I knew I had a good score. I can't tell you how happy I am with the way I was able to control my emotions when the pressure was on, not least of all when I birdied the last hole by sinking a 25 ft putt with my eyes closed!"

SCORING

All my research over the past 18 years or more has been dedicated to looking at a golfer's internal state (mind-body connection) in the moments *before* they take their shot, as the quality of this inner focus – a form of relaxed readiness or quiet concentration – determines, far more than knowledge of swing technique, the outcome of the shot.

The secret to effortless golf all comes down to how well you can connect your mind to your body in the gap or pause before movement commences. If you wiggle or waggle or do a little forward press with your hands before initiating your backswing, the rule still applies to the start of the actual swing; the rest you can consider as part of your personal shot preparation.

It's this ability to be really *present* in your breathing and your body that encourages fluidity of movement, not a head full of swing thoughts (or even positive thinking), which simply can't give you this same experience, but will in fact hinder your ability to bring your mind and body in sync and allow the motion of your shot to flow.

TRY THIS:

Score yourself from 1 to 10 on how well you can do the following during your next round of golf: 1 = Poor and 10 = Excellent

- Get into the relaxation response before each shot.

- Observe how the quality of your breathing affects your swing.

- Focus on the process and let the outcome take care of itself.

- Feel your grip pressure change depending on how you are breathing.

- Really be aware of your feet on the ground at address.

- Catch yourself rushing, and deliberately slow down.

- Notice how your common swing faults relate to your breathing.

- Play the game one breath, one shot and one hole at a time.

- Feel and let go of tension as you step on to the greens.

- Use your breathing to regroup and let go of any poor shots.

PART FIVE

PREPARING TO COMPETE

*"Regulate the breathing, and
thereby control the mind."*

BKS Iyengar

PRE-TOURNAMENT NERVES

For many golfers, pre-tournament nerves can start anywhere up to three weeks before a competition; they are the bane of a competitor's life and wreak havoc with eating and sleeping patterns, family and other relationships, practice time and the all-important preparation for the competition.

What's happening here? The mind has a life of its own and when unchecked will run rampant. Our training is to focus on the breathing, following the inhalation and exhalation of air, the purest, simplest and most fundamental of all our activities – the very thing that is keeping us alive.

Any time we come away from our breathing we go into the mind, into the realm of mechanical thinking (most of our thoughts have been thought before); we get on to the hamster wheel of our internal dialogue and go round and round incessantly, a slave to memories and imagination. The danger is that we disappear into these thoughts.

Research tells us that 80% of our thinking is negative. We are usually berating ourselves, telling ourselves why we can't do something, how we're going to fail or that we'll make a fool of ourselves if we even try. Your pre-tournament nerves begin and end with all these negative images you have in your mind around failure or at the very least not doing your best. You may worry about letting yourself down, as well as disappointing your family, your spouse, your coach and maybe even your sponsors and, worst of all, that you run the risk of looking like an idiot if your game falls apart or you choke.

These images can be based on reality (going over an actual incident where you shanked it off the first tee) or they can be imagined (what if I shank it off the first tee?). But whatever these thoughts and images are and wherever they originate (memory or imagination), they are taking you away from being in the *now*. All the training you've done is for one thing alone: to bring you back to the present moment, when you are *present* the mind and body can relate to help you produce the shot you want to make.

When you bring your attention to your breathing, all the words and pictures in your mind quieten down and some space is created inside your head, a space to be still, a pause to get centred, a vital moment in which you can settle over the ball.

Remember the sensory feedback loop? At its root, anxiety is a biochemical reaction in the nervous system, caused by shallow breathing – that is, taking small, short breaths into your upper chest, filling only the tops of your lungs with vital oxygen and nutrients to support your life. Incorrect breathing activates anxiety, as it flips a switch that sends you into the stress response. This reaction is completely dependent on your breathing and can be reversed (getting to neutral, or better yet, relaxation) only in the same way. However, it seems we just can't help getting involved (mind and emotions) and end up making the situation a thousand times worse.

Because you start to feel anxious (as a result of changes in the brain chemistry), the mind wants to support these feelings (as the thinking part of the mind is always trying to prove its own reality). It will create images and stories to justify all the reasons why you should be nervous, which then forces the emotions into a downward spiral, again in an attempt at cohesion, to support the feelings of anxiety.

Yet when you stay with the breathing, following it for the full in-breath and full out-breath, it can help you connect with your body, quieten the mind and calm the emotions.

The mental game, while extremely beneficial for goal-setting and enhancing self-esteem, cannot get to the root cause of anxiety before and during performance without working in conjunction with the breath. On its own, psychology can give you different words and pictures for your mind to work with, which might lead you to the doorway of the zone, but only a commitment to meditation can open the door and get you through to the actual experience.

Moving away from a reliance on mental game techniques alone requires vigilance (you need to see your own mind and how difficult it is to regulate the attention) and effort (to commit to your daily practice, follow the breath, and bring mind and body together).

Keep things as simple as possible in the weeks leading up to the tournament and just observe the changes that take place, including all your emotions, anxiety, irritation, pent up feelings, tightness and so on. This will be really good training for when you're actually on course and the anxiety and biochemical changes come up again when you're standing over the ball.

Observation creates distance (that space again) between yourself and your emotions and thoughts and activates that part of you which can be neutral and maintain inner detachment.

TRY THIS:

- Practise 15 to 20 minutes of meditation twice a day. Remember not to worry about getting it right, forcing or controlling your breath, analysing your practice or looking for results — just do your training.

- Self-observation: use your training journal to record what you notice about your own mind, for example, the times your imagination gets the better of you with negative images of losing. Again, don't try to change anything; just see it and bring yourself back to your breathing.

- Write down all your greatest shots, wins and triumphs — the times you turned it all around or came from behind to hole out and win over your competitors. Recall, if you can, the internal state you were in *before* hitting your best shots.

- Practise five minutes of visualisation following your meditation sessions or when doing something active like walking in nature or working out in the gym; see yourself again and again breathing deeply, feeling relaxed yet energised and quietly confident, minus thoughts, worries and anxiety.

- Ponder on these words of GI Gurdjieff, who advised his pupils to "Make everything quiet inside."

'Mind Full Golfer'
Image courtesy of Dennis Clark, PGA Master Professional, GolfWRX.com

THE NIGHT BEFORE

Preparation is everything. If you've prepared well over the previous weeks and months, using vigilant observation and continual effort – I said this training is simple but not easy – you will approach the night before the tournament in a cheerful, relaxed and positive state. When anxiety does show up, not only will you be able to see it for what it is (a biochemical reaction to shallow breathing), you'll also know exactly how to counter it and get back into flow.

There is constancy to this training: it is always the same, whether you're at home, on the driving range, walking out to the first tee, playing for position on the seventh fairway or preparing to sink an eagle putt on the 18th green.

The continual focus on the breath builds your attention, placing you in the here and now, minus mental interference; it is not a psychological technique but a practice – and the more you practise, the more prepared you are and the more you'll be able to stay calm and perform at your best under the pressure to come.

I worked for a brief time with a young professional golfer who, while he had enormous potential, suffered with nerves and had missed the cut on his last few tournaments. His management company, desperate to help him overcome the disastrous effects of adrenaline and anxiety, asked me to assist him, which I did.

As a young, up-and-coming golfer-athlete, Thriston had a great work ethic and took to the meditation training instantly, incorporating it into his daily routine and his preparation to compete. After just a few days practising, he teed up in another tournament, shot seven birdies in a row and broke the course record.

Spectacular things do happen when the mind and body can finally relate and you get yourself out of the way. Knowing that you have these skills, and that you've trained them and can rely on them, is crucial to your success.

TRY THIS:

- Remember not to look for the 'perfect' place to do your practice; sitting on the edge of the bath is fine, if that's the only quiet place in the house.

- Follow up your meditation practice by 'checking in' with yourself at various times during the day for a 'short burst' of several minutes or a few deep breaths.

- The night before a competition, it is usually quite difficult to sleep. Instead of lying there worrying, get out of bed and practise meditation to restore a calm state of mind. In the morning, practise meditation for 15 to 20 minutes immediately upon getting up. From then on, do short bursts of meditation to help reduce anxiety and maintain focus until the tournament. As your tee-off time approaches, these 'bursts' of meditation should be more frequent.

IN THE LOCKER ROOM

Review the chapter on 'Dividing Your Attention' (p102), as you will need to use this approach when you're in the locker room getting ready to tee off.

Remember, we're breathing every moment, but as soon as we get lost in our thoughts or emotions we simply forget. So try to maintain some awareness of your breathing, however slight and however tenuous, when you're lacing up your shoes, checking your bag, even when talking with others who are competing in the same tournament.

The more you've practised this in your everyday life, the more often you'll remember and the more you'll be reminded by your body and the breath also, as if from a very deep and knowing part of yourself.

Continue with your short bursts of meditation, which can last two to three minutes or even for a few deep breaths. As you sit and compose yourself, you'll be reminded by your upright posture of all the time you've spent training and how the inner quiet and mental space you've experienced in your practice will appear as a natural result of following the in-breath and the out-breath with your attention.

It's a foolproof method, so rely on it, remembering not to try and take deep breaths as this is counterproductive, but just keep your awareness on the lower abdomen (t'an tien), which will encourage the breath to deepen and slow down.

TRY THIS:

- Use short bursts of deep, slow and horizontal breathing as a way to encourage the meditative state to occur within you, so that you are relaxed yet focused for the competition ahead.

- Aim to divide your attention so you can continue to focus on your breathing while going through your usual pre-tournament routine, putting on your kit and tying your golf shoelaces.

- It is often particularly useful to concentrate the attention at the t'an tien, which will help to centre you physically and emotionally and produce a strong feeling of stability in your lower body. Some students have even reported that this helps them to master their body language as they walk out to the first tee, so that they look confident without getting the ego over-involved, but stay with the calmness of a quiet mind and emotional detachment.

WALKING TO THE FIRST TEE

In the eastern martial and spiritual arts, attention is paid to the simplest of things, like breathing, sitting, standing and walking: our so-called ordinary activities. However, once the focus of the practitioner is slowed down and brought into the present moment – following this breath, paying attention to physical sensation in this moment, being in this single footstep – things that once seemed ordinary are revealed as truly profound.

The root teaching of mindfulness, the essence of Buddhism, included mindfulness of the body, mindfulness of feelings and sensations, mindfulness of thoughts passing through the mind and mindfulness of Dharma (right living). The central tenet or one core discipline that the Buddha advocated above all others was mindfulness of breathing. *Breath-centred meditation by itself reveals to us the truth of the body, the feelings, the mind, and mental phenomena.*

Although it has been popularised and become the latest buzzword in everything from business to health, for the most part mindfulness has been separated from its Buddhist origins, as the essential teaching was given after Gautama Buddha attained enlightenment in order to help all sentient beings end suffering by learning detachment from grasping and craving by simply being in the here and now.

As I've mentioned many times in this book, and as you may well have noticed if you've been sincere with your practice, it is almost impossible to stay in the present moment, so scattered is the mind and the attention when left to its own devices.

It's only by noticing this tendency (which must to some extent be humbling) and making a concerted and consistent effort to hone and train the attention by following the breath that we can quieten down the internal dialogue and stay with the impression of ourselves in this moment.

TRY THIS:

- As you walk out to the first tee, observe the mental chatter and the beginnings of anxiety, which are natural reactions when faced with a stressful situation. Notice your surroundings and open your senses to the sky, the trees, the birds in the air and the earth beneath you.

- Expand your peripheral vision to include as much of the horizon as possible; this helps to activate the occipital lobe, which is responsible for producing the alpha brainwaves that will help get you into flow.

- Enjoy the quiet confidence that comes from breathing deeply and remaining detached from external factors, releasing you from feeling self-conscious or anxious, especially about other people and what they may think.

SETTING UP

The ability to stay in the present moment is nowhere more crucial than when setting up for your shot. If you can stay with your breathing here, you'll make a smooth and fluid swing, but if you let your nerves, mind or your ego get the better of you, it won't matter how much you know about technique – it simply won't come together, as your mind and body will be poles apart.

Staying in the present moment is vital and it's possible only when your mind is quiet. There is no other way to experience being in the now, than when the internal dialogue ceases, and this is best attained by following the breath.

Pay particular attention to your internal state when you're at address. If you're thinking about the shots you've already played or are worried about how many birdies you need to make over the remaining holes, you are no longer in the present, but either in the past or future.

It's highly likely that your thoughts and emotions, once excited in this way, will make you rush your preparation in an anxious attempt to force the ideal shot.

Golfers and other athletes who've experienced the zone or flow always report the same thing: time itself seems to slow down and they have all the time they need to prepare and execute movement without feeling stressed or hurried.

When you feel yourself rushing, simply slow down, step to one side and do short bursts of meditation, like my student Diane.

At the time Diane was fairly new to golf and was playing off 24. During a particular club competition where she was the captain of her team, the responsibility for keeping their one-shot lead and winning the match would be determined by how well she performed on the 18th – in particular by how she teed off to begin playing the final hole.

Understandably nervous, Diane stepped away to the side of the course while her playing partners took it in turn to tee off. Standing quietly with her hands pressed against her lower abdomen (t'an tien) she brought her focus into the present moment, noticing the anxiety she was feeling and the beginnings of mental interference, but simply followed her in-breaths and her out-breaths one after another until she felt her equilibrium restored.

She did the same thing later on in the clubhouse to keep her emotions under control when holding up the trophy and delivering her victory speech.

TRY THIS:

- **Kung Fu Set-Up Procedure**

  Remember that research shows it is possible for human beings to be 'in the present moment' for approximately 12 seconds: this is the perfect duration for your set-up and swing (or putting stroke) as it gives you the precise amount of time in which to bring mind and body together and activate 'the zone'.

  Practise at home or on the range to get your timing right and develop a more seamless transition between stillness and motion.

  At address, allow yourself 10 seconds to prepare for the shot and two seconds to swing (the average duration is between 1.5 and 1.8 seconds) using the following actions from Tai Chi to achieve a state of relaxed athleticism:

  i.   Empty your chest and loosen your shoulders.

  ii. Lower your awareness and your breathing to your t'an tien (centre of gravity).

  iii. Feel your weight in your footprints.

  Have you seen those old Brue Lee movies in which he would seem to compress himself into the ground before exploding with his famous one-inch punch? Well, this is what you're aiming for: notice that as you empty the upper body of tension, a firmer connection is established with the ground, which creates more stability and power.

Here's another kung fu essential that can help deliver between 20% and 30% more energy through the target:

iv. Simply inhale as you take the club away *slowly*... then breathe out as you move through impact and to your finish position.

If you can discipline your mind and body to master the 12-second rule each time you set up and swing, you'll play a more consistent game and deliver more effortless golf shots.

NB. As with all the breathing drills given, you must ensure that your attention is on your navel area (t'an tien), to encourage the breath to deepen; attempting these exercises with shallow breathing will have the opposite effect to that desired.

As Nicky Lawrenson LPGA observed when she attended one of my workshops, wherever you're breathing from tends to lead the movement, thus if you're breathing into the lower abdomen, the lower part of the body (hips and waist) will lead the swing motion while shallow breathing into the chest encourages the upper body to disconnect from the lower body and initiate the swing. Well spotted, Nicky!

PART SIX

IN CONTENTION

*"Breathe and be one with the air
that you breathe.*

*Breathe and be one with the river
that flows.*

*Breathe and be one with the earth
that you tread."*

Sister Annabel Laity

STAYING NEUTRAL

Left to their own devices, the mind and the emotions will take it in turns to get the better of you and distract you from focusing on your breathing – the mind with its relentless mental chatter, and the emotions with their wide-ranging spectrum constantly changing from excitement to anxiety and from frustration to joy.

In the blink of an eye, we are carried away from the present moment as the mind or the emotions seek to dominate our internal state, breaking the delicate thread of our attention, taking us away from our breathing and disrupting the communication between our mind and body.

Being neutral requires that you stay with your breathing so that this simple, one-pointed awareness is stronger than your thoughts and stronger than your emotions. Only then can you attain neutrality, be in the present moment and let your physical movement flow.

This is much easier said than done, which is why your daily sitting is so important and why taking time to incorporate breathing into your practice swings, pre-shot routine and so forth is essential. When we are sitting quietly in meditation it's difficult enough to follow the breath, as the mind is naturally restless, but it is possible to hone the attention to some degree with persistent effort and practice.

However, when the body is in motion and performing even the simplest of tasks, we tend to forget about the breath, and either try too hard to be in control or, if it's something we're familiar with, we switch to autopilot. Rarely, if ever, do we stay in the now, and simply follow the movement with a quiet mind.

There is no better example of trying too hard than when faced with the prospect of hitting a golf ball. In this scenario, the mind is usually full of swing thoughts, tips and tricks and technical information, leading to a breakdown in the mind-body connection, which results in a duff shot, usually followed by an emotional outburst such as anger.

Driving the car is a great example of being on autopilot, where the actions such as steering and changing gear can become automatic, letting the mind and emotions run free. You're behind the wheel, but are still reliving in your imagination that fabulous tee shot you played earlier or you're getting increasingly annoyed remembering the group behind who insisted on playing through and put you off your rhythm.

Breath-centred meditation is the ultimate training for keeping your attention where you are and on what you're doing. On the golf course, it is absolutely vital that you are composed, neutral and don't disappear into your mind or your emotions but stay *present* with the shot you're taking.

TRY THIS:

- Neutrality requires that whatever happens, your focus stays the same and doesn't deviate; thus you should try to regroup as often as you can throughout the game, following your breath continually to quieten the mind, control your biochemistry, restore equilibrium and allow your movement to flow.

- Work with the **Chi-Performance GOLF** mantra, "One breath at a time, one shot at a time, one hole at a time" to keep your focus in the moment.

- Any time you feel yourself getting excited or irritated, remember that a short burst of meditation (a few deep breaths into the navel area) can reactivate the inner condition of relaxed concentration, the ideal state from which to play your best shots.

> • If you work with a caddie, have him or her remind you often about your breathing. If you can encourage them to meditate or do a few practice sessions together pre-tournament, even better. The resulting entrainment or synergy between you will pay dividends when you're under pressure.

HANDLING PRESSURE

High-pressure moments are when you really need to commit to following the breath and not revert back to being too technical or abandoning the practice altogether because you want more (perceived) control, are desperate to make the shot happen, and believe in some way that you can manage this all by yourself.

If you've been practising self-observation, you will have seen just how often you forget your breathing, and you will have noticed too that during your meditation sessions (especially when first starting the practice) you couldn't help but interfere with, control and organise the breath rather than simply allowing a full and complete inhalation and exhalation without your ego (which always thinks it knows better) getting involved.

When you see this and can acknowledge it as fundamentally true, then you will see how it applies to most other things in your life. It certainly applies to golf – trying too hard, thinking too much, wanting to have control, thinking your way through technical points, organising swing mechanics, trying to make it happen. Yet every story we've ever heard of, the perfect golf shot from the game's elite to the everyday player, one golfer after another recounts that they weren't thinking too much, nor trying too hard and that the shot itself was effortless.

This is what needs to be recreated in the moments before you start moving: a quiet mind (not thinking too much); a relaxed attention both mentally and physically (not trying too hard); and a freedom of movement (effortlessness) that occurs when mind and body work together.

Conversely, what the mainstream culture of golf asks you to do is continue interfering with and overriding the innate wisdom of the mind-body connection, to try to control, analyse and organise the 1.5 to 1.8 seconds of one of the most complex movements in all sport. Yet handling pressure requires just the opposite: it entails getting out of your own way and trusting this superior intelligence and that is possible only when you relinquish control.

The shot needs something from you, of course: it needs your passion for the game, and it needs a certain level of skill (approximately three years of learning), but it also needs the central intelligence of the mind-body connection to help movement flow. This can be accomplished only via the vehicle of your breath, without your mental chatter blocking the line.

TRY THIS:

- Rather than trying to force the pressure shot, see how your breath comes up to the chest at the same time that your mind starts with all the technical thoughts and your body becomes tight. Simply reverse these symptoms by following the breath until it is deep and slow; only then should you take your shot.

POSITIVE ACCEPTANCE

After 19 years of playing professional golf and competing in 74 Majors, 37-year-old Sergio Garcia finally won The Masters at Augusta, Georgia on 9 April 2017.

Let's be honest, we all thought it was going to be Justin Rose's day as the Olympic and former Open Champion was certainly seen as having the best chance, the cooler head and the most even temperament going into the last round.

But the crowds and patrons and the fans on social media as well as the golfing gods were rooting for Garcia that day, and here's why.

It's not just my Spanish ancestry that makes me feel proud to say this, and it's not just because it would have been Seve Ballesteros' 60th birthday that made Sergio's win the more poignant – it was because we saw real Mediterranean-style passion on the golf course, but passion tamed through perseverance and acceptance, which finally distilled as sheer self-belief.

Even the missed opportunities, the wayward shots and the stray putts couldn't shake Garcia's conviction or his inner calm as he came back again and again under the most intense pressure, without giving in to his sometimes tetchy emotions and self-berating, self-defeating attitude.

Instead he decided to accept fate and keep fighting back.

Indeed, Sunday's back nine were like a microcosm of Garcia's entire career, ending in a resounding victory as he closed like a champion on the course he found most troubling, and he did it by coming back from two down with five to go, against a steely nerved Major winner and gold medallist.

At the play-off at 18, Garcia needed to two-putt for par from 12 ft. He got there in one. In his interview shortly before accepting the Green Jacket from the previous year's winner, Danny Willett, Garcia explained how he'd felt during the day:

"I was very calm, much calmer than yesterday, much calmer than I've felt probably in any major championship on Sunday. Obviously Justin wasn't making it easy. He was playing extremely well. But I knew what I was capable of doing, and I believed that I could do it. Thanks to that, I was able to do it."

After years of battling with the course he'd found the most challenging of all, Garcia finally got around to accepting that Augusta can give and that it can take away. This ability to accept outcomes and just keep playing the next shot and the next, ultimately led to victory.

Bravo Sergio!

BETWEEN SHOTS

The practice of walking meditation, known as Kinhin, is traditionally practised between long periods of seated meditation (Zen). If time and space allows for you to do this after your daily practice, you can learn to bring some of this enhanced awareness to your game as you walk between shots.

WALKING MEDITATION

Aim to walk back and forth along the same path or in a circle, preferably outside in nature but definitely away from heavily built-up areas and the noise of traffic. Before you start walking, stand quietly for a few minutes, breathing deeply and bringing your attention to your body, noticing how your body feels and any physical sensations.

When you start walking, go slowly so that your pace is steady and even and you can stay with each step as you take it, one step after another. You are not intending to go anywhere or arrive at a destination, and there is nothing to achieve except the experience of relaxed concentration and being in the present moment.

Simply stay with the process and just walk slowly, carefully and with your full awareness on your breathing and your footsteps for 10 to 15 minutes.

TRY THIS:

- Relax your face, shoulders and chest and bring your attention to your navel area (t'an tien), taking long, slow, deep breaths as you walk to the tee.

- Rather than buying into your mental chatter and the biochemical reactions that trigger anxiety, keep your attention on your breathing, staying aware of the sensation of your feet on the ground, one step after another as you walk to the next shot.

- Know that everything is coming together the way it should and that so long as you continue to follow your breathing and stay with the sensation of walking, your mind and body will get in sync as a natural result of this sincere effort.

- If for any reason your shot goes awry, start over on the next walk to the ball.

REFOCUSING

If you've been involved in business or commerce, you may be familiar with the work of Werner Erhard, the American critical thinker and creator of transformational models for individuals and organisations.

One of Erhard's leading ideas is that of the 'Occurring World', which he explains thus:

"The Occurring World includes the way in which objects, others, and you yourself occur for you in this or that situation. It is the world you live in, the one you respond to or react to. Our way of being and our actions are a correlate of the way in which the circumstances we are dealing with occur (show up) for us."

If you're into popular philosophical concepts like the New Age, you may be more familiar with the 'Law of Attraction', which similarly states that we attract to our reality a match to what we're thinking and feeling at any given moment as the magnetic power of the universe draws similar energies together. It manifests itself in an individual's life by drawing to them ideas of a similar kind, people who are alike in outlook and temperament, and also situations and circumstances that correspond to one's expectations.

Can you take advantage of the Occurring World and the Law of Attraction in your golf game? Yes, you can, simply by adopting an attitude of positive acceptance, similar to Garcia's when he won the Masters Tournament in 2017.

This approach tells us to act powerfully, while acknowledging any uncomfortable feelings and even accepting negative outcomes, while allowing the world to keep on occurring in a positive way because that's what we choose to focus on.

It's the best way to regroup on-course and coupled with your short bursts of meditation it will help you to clear your mind and think only those thoughts that are helpful to you and your performance.

Here's a great example from the amazing Jack Nicklaus, whose way of thinking about golf was truly exceptional. Playing on the PGA Tour with Australian golfer Jack Newton, who had just mishit an easy shot, Nicklaus remarked, "But Jack, that's the best shot you could have played!"

Always focused on the positive, this remark just about sums up Nicklaus's approach to the mental aspect of the game and is a great example of how the world and golf occur according to your mindset.

A little closer to your own game perhaps, is this feedback I received from one of my long-term students, Tim, who at the time was a 5-handicap player:

"Hi Jayne, I had a really interesting insight into the occurring world last week. I played in an 'Open' 36-hole competition event at my local club and for some reason I just couldn't get negative thoughts out of my head leading up to it and hey presto, the world did occur as very difficult in the morning round! I was very tense and played accordingly!

"At lunchtime I wandered over with a few balls to the practice ground, which has beautiful views over the marshes and a river estuary and thought that I would be really happy just to sit and gaze at the view for the rest of the afternoon. I then did a few minutes of standing meditation according to your instructions and suddenly seemed much calmer and accepted that I could handle whatever came my way in the afternoon round and was not going to ruin a beautiful few hours on a lovely sunny day!

"Needless to say, I played really well in the afternoon and got myself into a really strong position before a couple of really tough breaks came my way late on and I only missed out on winning by a handful of shots having been almost last out of 54 players after the morning round. I still managed to post the best score in the afternoon, which was great, but not as valuable as the lesson I learned!"

For now, simply regroup any time you need to by taking yourself off to one side and tuning into the rhythm of your breathing, following each inhalation and exhalation completely, without getting lost in the chattering of your mind.

Refocusing is about getting back to the process which allows for an effortless shot to occur, that is, working your mind-body connection. It is not about going over technical thoughts in your head or fiddling about, searching for a swing. That just takes you into the analytical mind, which, if employed when swinging a golf club, serves only to delay the signal about your intended movement from reaching the motor system. No matter how much you know about golf swing mechanics, the result will be a clumsy, ineffective shot.

TRY THIS:

- Always reach for the flow state of 'relaxed concentration' by using deep, slow breathing to quieten your mind and get you back in the present moment.

- Act positively, no matter what has just occurred. Focus on your attitude and detach from negative thoughts and feelings by following your breath, remembering that whatever the outcome, it was the best shot you could have played.

INSTINCT AND INTUITION

You may remember Graeme McDowell's 15 ft putt to win the final singles match at Celtic Manor, securing victory for Team Europe during the 2010 Ryder Cup.

Fresh from his US Open victory, McDowell led by three shots early on but dropped back to one up with three holes to play after driving into heavy rough left of the green and then duffing his chip shot on the 15th. However, he recovered brilliantly to hole a nail-biting 15 ft putt to win the 16th, leaving Hunter Mahan unable to respond for Team USA on the 17th, conceding the hole as his chip landed just short of the green.

When interviewed after the tournament, 'Gmac' said he was so nervous before taking that crucial putt that he could hardly even feel his hands, his adrenaline was pumping so much. In that moment of absolute pressure, with the eyes of the golfing world watching, he said, "It all came down to instinct and intuition."

It will be exactly the same for you next time the responsibility for landing the winning shot is in your hands, whether it's a major tournament or a club medal championship: the nervous system knows no difference between Amen Corner and the water hazard at your local course.

Thinking your way through any pressure scenario spells disaster, yet instinct and intuition, (the soft skills that are needed to perform in these situations) are so often overridden by the analytical mind, which wants to have control. Added to this is the fact that the mainstream approach to the game has given the mind so much credence that the majority of golfers have difficulty playing to their potential because they are overloaded with mechanical data and mental game techniques that are believed to be the only things to fall back on.

So how do you develop your instinct and intuition so that you can rely on it during pressure shots? You guessed it: with breath-centred meditation.

Here's why.

When you go about your everyday life, you are operating in the beta state; this is the brainwave pattern that allows the mind to be alert, think rationally, tackle goals and organise tasks. Most people are in the beta state all day long, which is fine for going through your to-do list, but it spells disaster for executing a fluid golf shot, especially under pressure.

Being in the beta state makes it difficult to access instinct, intuition and creativity, as the only thing we have at our disposal in this state is the mind's own input, that is, the constant churning of the internal dialogue, the mechanical and mostly unconscious stream of thoughts endlessly revolving as we talk to ourselves throughout the day.

As I've said elsewhere, mental game problems cannot be resolved on the same level at which they are created; instead what's needed is to get beyond the logical, analytical and rational mind and into another realm.

Meditation encourages the production of alpha brainwaves, which give us access to instinct and intuition and other realms beyond the rational mind, such as touch, feel and sensitivity.

Correct breathing on the golf course (i.e. the applied meditative state) allows you to have a more unified experience of yourself; it unites left- and right-brain hemispheres (the logical and intuitive respectively), lighting up the whole brain, giving you access to the present moment and to the elusive state where mind and body work as one.

It also negates the power of negative emotions and helps to create the ideal performance state, balanced between tension and relaxation, between trying and not trying too hard.

The dictionary tells us that intuition is the ability to understand something from knowing rather than reasoning, that is, a gut feeling or hunch. Often intuition is instantaneous in nature, an insight that gives immediate knowledge and a multilayered depth of understanding.

A typical example of this would be on the greens. When a golfer is in the zone (alpha state or Zen-mind), they are able to read the undulations of the putting surface instantly and know instinctively how to play the shot. In this coveted state of relaxed concentration, they stay with these first impressions, without over-thinking, and commit to what their instincts tell them.

Counter to this is the golfer who steps on to the green in a state of anxiety and rather than experiencing a momentary flash of insight of how best to make the putt, they employ the logical mind to work it out. But the shallow breathing, nervousness and feelings of stress mean they second-guess themselves, anxiously looking at the hole again and again, rushing their preparation and ultimately duffing the shot, as the mind and body are out of sync.

So intuition is not thinking 'about' something but is more akin to receiving knowledge; this is only possible when the usually solid wall of the mind (which always wants to 'know') becomes quiet, peaceful and non-grasping and allows access to a deeper level that can see and sense and feel – and you know how to train this by now.

What's truly remarkable is that of all the creatures on this planet, we are the only ones who can be conscious of our breathing. Just think about that for a minute, while gently following your breath.

By becoming conscious of our breathing and training ourselves to stay with the physical sensation of breathing in and breathing out, we can come to a place where silence reigns, intuition flows and where the fickleness of the mind and the changeability of the emotions are all but absent; this is a glimpse into the oneness of our original nature.

It is impossible to breathe deeply and slowly and have an agitated mind; it is impossible to breathe deeply and slowly and have a mind overcrowded with swing thoughts; it is impossible to breathe deeply and slowly and feel irritated or angry or have your nerves get the better of you on a decisive shot.

The most important thing – again – that you can do for your golf game and indeed your life, is to focus your attention on your breathing, first and foremost as a daily practice and then as often as you can remember throughout the day.

By so doing you can reduce mental interference, gain access to the zone or flow state, control your biochemistry (nerves and anxiety), activate the mind-body connection to help deliver fluid, powerful, effortless and precise golf shots and, moreover, you can maintain this exceptional level of performance under pressure.

Amazing!

TRY THIS:

- Enjoy the momentary stillness before executing your shot; allow yourself to take a few deep breaths every time you're at address to encourage your intuition about the shot to surface.

- Take your time: rushing is a sure sign you've come away from the present moment and out of the zone or flow. This is especially important when you're nervous, but if you can maintain the discipline to connect with your breathing you help to switch on the innate intelligence of the mind-body connection.

- Always remember that mental knowledge and fluidity of motion are unhappy bedfellows, as the former will always cancel out the latter. Use your rational mind (left brain) for learning and honing swing mechanics on the driving range and switch on the meditative state via slow, deep breathing on the golf course, coming into the realm of instinct, touch and feel (right brain).

The Buddha in Meditation

PART SEVEN

GOLF ENIGMAS

"The great mistake is to anticipate the outcome of the engagement; you ought not to be thinking of whether it ends in victory or defeat. Let nature take its course, and your tools will strike at the right moment."

Bruce Lee

PERFORMANCE PARADOXES

From my training, research and exploration over the past 31 years I've identified many paradoxes in relation to movement and performance. These paradoxes are like traps that even the best golfers and the most intelligent people can fall into.

In fact, the more you know about golf technically and the stronger your mind, the more difficulty you may have accepting these paradoxes as true, although chances are you've already seen them show up in your game.

PARADOX NO.1 – THE HARDER YOU TRY, THE WORSE IT GETS

This seems to ring true for anything connected with developing athletic potential, especially where the performance of movement under pressure is concerned.

There is a lovely story about a student just starting out on their Tai Chi journey who asked their master how long it would take for them to excel in the art. The master replied, "About 30 years." The student then asked, "But what if I practise twice as hard?" to which the master replied, "In that case, 50 years."

Remember when I talked about the qualities needed to approach this training?

You cannot bring your everyday self with you on this journey; or at least you can bring it along only as something to struggle with. The mind refuses point blank to give up its identification with what it thinks it knows and relinquish the mistaken belief that by a combination of knowledge and willpower it's possible to achieve greatness on the golf course.

Yet to be 'successful' (if indeed such a word can be used when adopting this eastern approach) we must only use our willpower to be consistent in our practice of meditation. By learning to be patient and quieten down the internal dialogue, we see that the effort needed is not so much an effort to accomplish something, but an effort simply to be where we are. You cannot force the meditative state or the zone into being, any more than you can force a good golf shot, especially when you most need to make it.

As the Japanese Kyudo master in Eugen Herrigel's famous book, *Zen in the Art of Archery*, tells him, "What stands in your way is that you have too much wilful will. You think that what you do not do yourself does not happen."

PARADOX NO.2 – TRAINING A PATTERN IS COUNTER TO EFFORTLESS MOTION

We've already talked briefly about how Murphy's law (p71) comes into play when dealing with the technical nature of the 'golfing machine': the fact that in a complex sequence such as the golf swing, which involves a variety of moving parts, if something can go wrong it's inevitable that it will go wrong.

Let's take another quick look at what the world's most famous kung fu fighter, Bruce Lee, brought to our understanding of movement and (as per the title of one of his books) *The Art of Expressing the Human Body*.

Lee's extensive research into the martial arts led him to believe that each system is fundamentally flawed or at least has its own weaknesses. He therefore developed his unique 'way without a way', Jeet Kune Do, as an amalgamation of the best of all the fighting arts, which included boxing (he was heavily influenced by Muhammad Ali), Wing Chun (his early teacher was grandmaster Ip Man) and fencing (from which he developed his famous lunge punch).

The trouble with a method or style, according to Lee, is that it traps the user in a pattern, a routine, or a tradition and as such it offers but a shadow of understanding rather than empowering the individual with the ability to move freely and naturally in the moment.

If you've read *Extraordinary Golf*, you'll recall that the number one thing Shoemaker's years of coaching have taught him is that all golfers really want from the game is this same sense of freedom. He says, "When letting go becomes more important than the quality of your shots, the quality of your shots will amaze you."

Overarching the performance of complex physical movement is the necessity for internal stillness: the relaxed but ready stance of history's greatest warriors. Endlessly going over your swing technique on the driving range defies this law; and this helps explain why even the most experienced player can have a beautiful, languid swing in practice, but being constrained by knowledge rather than feeling free when standing over the ball, they will hit it fat, slice it or leave it short on the greens.

Above all, your daily meditation can help you train this coveted experience of relaxed readiness; a state that is attainable only by focusing on the breath and bringing mind and body together as one.

PARADOX NO.3 – TO OBTAIN THE DESIRED OUTCOME, FOCUS ON THE PROCESS

Focusing on the process hones your ability to stay *present* and aware for the duration of your swing. This aim can best be served by using the breath, which is the one true constant evident before, during and after each shot. This is the way to consistency and the game of effortless golf; unfortunately it's not the game most people are playing when they're on the golf course.

The trouble with our attention, which could also be described as awareness, for what we're aware of we give our attention to, is that it flickers hither and yon so that we cannot stay with one thought or one focus for anything more than fractions of a minute. Swing thoughts change, moods change and mental focus comes and goes.

Fred Shoemaker writes about how the mind of every golfer jumps from one swing thought to another, and while you might get away with this on the driving range, the nervous tension and pressure during play and competition creates gaps, ie danger spots in your awareness where you are prey to changing your mind, losing focus, anticipating the outcome and letting in "fear, doubt, worry and muscle-tightening".

It's easy to understand how this natural tendency of the human mind, which is ever restless and often agitated, is simply exacerbated by the mainstream approach, which would have you 'think about moving' (swing technique) and 'think about thinking' (psychology and the mental game).

The best way to close the gaps in awareness, to stay focused and in the present moment, is to seek help beyond the ordinary level of the mind and the emotions, help from something that's constant and unwavering, something that you can depend on. That's right, your breathing; and keeping your awareness on the breath so that it helps activate your mind-body connection and seamlessly organise the complex chain of movement each time you prepare to swing.

Some time ago, I was working with an older PGA professional and even though Richard had been involved in the game as a coach and player for more than 60 years, he was astonished at the enhanced quality of his ball-striking when he began to practise meditation and use deep breathing as the anchor point of his game. Having more knowledge than most about swing mechanics, the one thing he needed was to be able to trust his body (that sense of freedom again) rather than simply relying on the information in his mind.

Maintaining his focus on the process of breathing, and staying with this awareness while going through his preparation, practice swings and visualisation of the shot, Richard was able to remove self-interference, activate a state of relaxed concentration and enhance the delivery of more pure golf shots.

He exemplified the words of Herrigel's Kyudo master, "He grows daily more capable of following any inspiration without technical effort, and also of letting inspiration come to him through meticulous observation."

EFFORT AND RESULTS

The purpose of this book has been to explore the relationship between your breathing, the ability to quieten your mind, neutralise anxiety, enhance the fluidity of movement and ultimately win more golf competitions.

The single most important factor in helping you to accomplish this and achieve a level of play that will be joyful, satisfying and sometimes perhaps even astonishing is the consistent practice of formal breath-centred meditation, the centuries-old teaching that is fundamental to the Buddhist tradition.

Our breath is given to us when we are born and our last breath will be taken just moments before we die. In between times, if we can somehow train ourselves to remember the fact that we are breathing, our everyday life will take on a different quality as we see the fragility of our state and acknowledge that on our own we can do nothing. We can pursue our goals and aims and ambitions only so long as our breath remains. Focusing on the breath, we bring the mind and body together and are invited into the present moment, and the experience of being in the now.

Making effort towards the daily practice of sitting quietly following your breathing for 15 to 20 minutes will help in all areas of your life and will notably serve to help recreate the internal conditions needed for the perfect shot to manifest itself on the golf course. This is not philosophy, but a deep and purposeful practice and establishes the correct order of things allowing for a transformation to occur in your game.

Breathing correctly enhances the mind-body connection and primes your inner state such that the zone can manifest itself; this in turn enables complex movement to flow, as the self-interference that normally hinders the communication between the brain's motor system and your neurons, tendons, and muscle fibres is minimised.

Overworking your swing technique, thinking too much and trying too hard cancels out the delicate balance between mind and body as the ego, fear and anxiety wreak havoc with this internal connection by overriding the subtlety and simplicity of the meditative state.

However, the right kind of effort – training your ability to be quiet and in the present moment – will help reproduce the conditions we know from long research and study are apparent within every golfer from tour pro to committed amateur in the moments before they hit an effortless shot.

Students who have committed to the practice report one victory after another, from their first ever eagle putt, to the winning of interclub, pro-am and tour events. But still the paradoxes continue: you cannot do this training in order to win at golf, although with dedicated and consistent training, it's highly likely you will be a champion.

BREATHING TO WIN

The Buddha did not bring us the practice of meditation so we could improve our golf games, lift trophies and give rousing victory speeches in the clubhouse. But in his infinite wisdom he showed us that by placing our attention on the breathing, we gain immediate access to the only constant thread that runs through our life, bypassing the malleable, fluctuating and impermanent inner world of our thoughts and emotions.

By now you will have started your practice and you will have picked up on the irony inherent in approaching this training in order to achieve something. Remarkably though, what can be gained through dedicated and sincere effort is the one thing most coveted by all sportspeople and performers the world over: the ability to access a state of relaxed concentration, allowing for fluidity yet precision of movement, the only attribute that separates the champion from the runner-up.

Yet you cannot meditate with this outcome in mind. By practising for personal gain, you'll come face to face with the ultimate contradiction, and the result will be counter to that desired. If, however, you commit with all sincerity and a little reverence for the practice itself, you will learn how to activate the right internal conditions that will allow you to beat your opponents, not just those in your own mind and heart, but those you're playing against on the course.

As you follow the way many others before you have taken, the practice of meditation and the applied meditative state through deep and purposeful breathing will be revealed as fundamental to all things. As one student said recently:

"I feel a shift occurring; I'm beginning to think of golf as part of my breathing practice rather than the other way around."

BIBLIOGRAPHY

Chadwick, David, *Crooked Cucumber; The Life and Zen Teaching of Shunryu Suzuki*, Thorsons, 1999

Gurdjieff, GI, *Views from the Real World*, Routledge and Keegan Paul, 1976

Hanh, Thich Nhat, *Breathe! You are Alive*, Translated by Annabel Laity, Rider, 1992

Herrigel, Eugen, *Zen in the Art of Archery*, Routledge and Kegan Paul, 1955

Lee, Bruce, *The Tao of Jeet Kune Do*, Ohara, 1975

Murphy, Michael, *Golf in the Kingdom*, Penguin Compass, 1997

Morris, Karl, *Attention! The Secret to You Playing Better Golf*, London Press, 2014

Shoemaker, Fred, *Extraordinary Golf*, Perigee, 1996

Suzuki, Shunryu, *Zen Mind, Beginner's Mind*, Weatherhill Press, 1970

RESOURCES I

THE MISSING LINK IN GOLF'S MENTAL GAME

FREE ONLINE VIDEO SERIES

To help with your daily practice and applications of breath-centred meditation when you're preparing for and playing competitive golf, Jayne has created three full-length video lessons, which you can view for free online.

Please search for the Chi-Power GOLF channel on YouTube to access the following:

  Part 1: Performance Breathing (6:48)

  Part 2: Relaxed Concentration (9:55)

  Part 3: Playing in the Zone (8:29)

If you leave a comment or question underneath the videos, Jayne will be sure to reply.

"Jayne, I really enjoyed your videos and your very low-key ways of sharing. For me your information is spot on and should be addressed with the pros as well as amateur golfers. Keep up what you are doing and look forward to working with you in the future."

Michael Hebron, PGA Hall of Fame

RESOURCES II

DEEP PRACTICE FOR EFFORTLESS GOLF

AUDIO PROGRAMME

Jayne Storey's entire method of **Chi-Performance GOLF** has been packaged in a unique three-part audio programme read by the author.

In *Deep Practice for Effortless Golf*, Jayne teaches you how to quieten your mind, control anxiety and work with your breathing to enter the zone of relaxed concentration.

You will also learn the biomechanical principles of Tai Chi, which, when applied to golf, can help you develop a relaxed athleticism, better balance and a more stable swing.

For more details, please visit

www.chi-performance.com/shop/

"Jayne very clearly debunks the myth that top athletes are experiencing 'adrenaline rush' when they start hitting the ball further than usual in the heat of competition. In fact, they are in the flow state of meditation or 'the zone'. The impact her coaching has had on my game in only a few short weeks is more significant than the last three years of gym work, practice and competing on average five days per week. The benefit, which she does not 'sell' or push on to you, is that I have gained significant power and accuracy through the combination of breathing and controlling my biomechanics. As someone over 40, to go from 100 mph to 105 mph in three years' working out to 112 mph through simple breathing techniques is nothing short of incredible. I highly recommend her audio programme to any golfer looking to reach their potential."

JPK, 4 hdcp, Hong Kong

RESOURCES III

CHI-PERFORMANCE GOLF
PERSONAL TUITION PROGRAMMES

The **Chi-Performance GOLF** method (established 2002) offers a unique approach to movement and performance enhancement in golf, based on strengthening the mind-body connection.

The method is founded on the martial arts and meditative traditions of the East, including Chi Kung (postural exercises), Tai Chi (a *soft-*style martial art) and Chan (Chinese Zen) meditation. These 'deep practices' are verified by the latest research in sports-science and neuroscience to help golfers unite mental game with technique, and access the zone or flow, more specifically to:

- overcome performance anxiety
- reduce mental interference
- control adrenaline
- deliver fluid, effortless shots
- excel in competition
- win medals and trophies.

Jayne Storey offers personal tuition at a number of prestigious golf clubs across the south-east of England. She also offers online tuition to students across the world.

To learn more about these programmes and to enquire about costs and availability, please contact Jayne via the website.

If you would like to enquire about Jayne presenting a talk or workshop at your golf club, please get in touch.

www.chi-performance.com/contact/

ABOUT THE AUTHOR

Jayne Storey is a pioneer of the emerging genre that seeks to unite eastern spiritual practice with high performance in pressure situations.

Her unique approach helps golfers strengthen their mind-body connection so they can bring together their mental game and technique to deliver fluid yet precise shots, especially during competition.

Jayne's expertise is based on a lifetime's 'deep practice' and teaching of Buddhist meditation and Tai Chi. Based on almost two decades of independent research and development, her unique **Chi-Performance GOLF** methodology is now proven across all levels of the game.

She writes for a number of industry publications and has been featured on BBC television and radio.

Jayne is a long-term member of the Tai Chi Union. An avid gym-goer, she loves circuit and interval training. When she's not working out she likes to read the Indian classic, *Bhagavad Gita*, play the guitar and spend time in Malta exploring her family history.

www.chi-performance.com

Printed in Great Britain
by Amazon